What is a
GOOD
MAN?

What is a
GOOD
MAN?

Waymond L. Burton III

What is a Good Man? by Waymond L. Burton III
Published by Equipping Ministries
Post Office Box 25446
Greenville, SC 29616

www.whatisagoodman.com
info@whatisagoodman.com

.

Unless otherwise noted, all Scripture quotations are from the *New King James Version* of the Bible.

ISBN-10: 0615580807
ISBN-13: 978-0-615-58080-7

Second Edition

This book is dedicated to my father, Bishop Waymond L. Burton, Jr., whose character, integrity, and faithfulness personifies the answer to the title of this book. He lives, teaches, and trains what it means to be a good man.

To my wife Camille, son Josiah, and daughter Jadyn who are my continual motivation to measure up to God's standard of a good man and whose patience with my failures and shortcomings deserve greater honor than I can give them.

Finally, to my Lord and Savior Jesus Christ who is my everything and without whom my life would have no purpose. The glory goes to You!

Contents

Endorsements

What is a Good Man? is a fascinating book and a must read for both women and men. Pastor Burton does an excellent job in defining what it means to be a good man according to the standards set forth in the word of God. I believe this book will be a blessing to men and women, both young and old.

Bishop Waymond L. Burton, Jr.
Senior Pastor
Zina Christian Center, Raleigh, North Carolina

This book will help women to know what men wish women knew about them and can be used in a weekly men's Bible study. I venture to say that everyone who reads this book will want to read parts of it again and again.

Pastor John R. Peyton, Ph.D.
Registered Christian Family Counselor and Therapist
Manassas, Virginia

In an era when normative rationale, roles, and reason of manhood are being redefined over and over again, Waymond Burton III contends: "No man is born a good man; he must become a good man." He gets straight to the business of examining twelve biblical verses paralleled with real life examples of the phrase "good man." This treatise is not intellectual quasi-babbling or discoursing; it is candid talk for any level reader. You are holding in your hand a timeless book for men, women, and children regardless of the context of the relationship with the men in your life. If you've got simple or tough questions, Waymond has proven and tested answers that will tackle and transform your male relationships!

Dr. Walter Boston, Jr.
Senior Team Leader
C.A.U.S.E. International
Charlotte, North Carolina

Acknowledgements

There are so many people who worked tirelessly on this project and I want to express my sincere thanks. My assistant Carolina Crunkelton labored greatly interpreting my subpar handwriting and typing the entire manuscript. There were two people I called on repeatedly to read, proof, and give feedback throughout the writing process - my spiritual daughter Danette "Tweedy" Poole and my sister Jeneen Baret. My wife Camille spent countless hours and used an abundance of red ink while editing the manuscript ensuring every detail was just right. I am also grateful to my father Bishop Waymond Burton, Jr. and my mentors Dr. John Peyton and Dr. Walter Boston, Jr. for reading, screening, and endorsing this book. All of your sacrifices have made this book possible. Thank you!

Foreword

The subject of this book begs the question, "Is this man qualified to write on this subject?" Well, if anyone can attest to whether or not Waymond is a "good man" as described in the scripture, it ought to be me. Waymond and I have been married for almost fifteen years. I think it safe to say that I am the one person who knows him best. I know him to be loyal. I know that I can trust him.

Why was I drawn to him? Aside from his outgoing nature, infectious smile, and genuine joyous laughter, it was obvious he was a man of conviction, integrity, and godly character. Does this mean that Waymond is perfect? Absolutely not! As you truly get to know someone you learn their weaknesses and their strengths. But is his heart perfect towards God? Absolutely!

My husband knew what God had called him to do before I ever entered his life. Therefore, if I wanted to be with him, I had to be willing to yield to whatever the Lord had called him to do because he was going to obey the Lord. In our case, it meant moving away from family to found and pastor a church. But, it was what the Lord ordered!

There have been times in our journey together in life and ministry that have been stressful, challenging, and even disappointing. I have seen my husband walk through many of those times. His character did not change. His loyalties did not change. I could still rely upon him to be dependable and faithful. But, it was in those times God continued to shape us and strip us of all the traits of our personalities that cause us not to be like Him. But, when we can get to the other side of our various trials with faith and favor, we have proven our trustworthiness to God.

As you read this book, let me put your questions to rest. According to the standard as set forth in these twelve verses in the Bible, Waymond L. Burton III is a good man!

Camille G. Burton
Waymond L. Burton III's wife

Introduction

The U.S. Marines regularly declare that they are looking for "a few good men." Posters have been printed by the military for years with Uncle Sam pointing forward and saying, "I want you." No doubt he is asking for good men. Every church in America needs good men. Many single women are saying, "I don't need a few, I just need one good man!" There are also some married women saying, "If my husband was a good man, my life would be complete." So many married women are discouraged because the one they are with does not measure up to what they think a good man should be.

The truth of the matter is good men are in great demand. People are searching many venues to find them. They find themselves seeking advice from books, newspapers, magazine articles, television, reality, and talk shows. These commentators give their opinion on the "how-to" of finding and keeping a good man. The notoriety of many of these commentators gathers a lot of support on their views of what is a good man.

Online dating websites and matchmaking services are in high demand. Someone can give their specifications and have matches returned based on that person's preferences. While there is nothing inherently wrong with dating websites, a man or woman must still choose his or her standards. One can even attempt to get more advice by searching www.howtofindagoodman.net.

The bigger question is really how to *identify* a good man rather than how to *find* a good man. Celebrities, experts, and everybody else have given their opinion on this particular subject. When the bottom line is this: how does God say we should identify a good man? What is a good man according to God's standards? Once this question has been answered, no one else's standard really matters.

Throughout the chapters of this book we're going to go through every verse in the Bible that uses the phrase "good man" and from them identify what a good man really is. If anyone knows what a good man is, it ought to be God. He is the creator of man and therefore the only one qualified to define a "good man."

If you were to ask most people what a good man is, they will give you their view based on their understanding of the word "good" in the phrase "good man." They may say he is friendly, honest, hard-working, charming, chivalrous, or strong. These are great qualities for any man to possess and may qualify him as a "nice guy." However, what's often overlooked is the non-negotiable quality that a "good man" should first be committed to God. No one is inherently "good" according to the Bible. Therefore, the Spirit of God is the irreplaceable ingredient of the word "good" in "good man." It distinguishes a "nice guy" from a "good man."

There are thirteen verses in the Bible that use the phrase "good man." Since two of those verses are exactly the same, I have combined them. Therefore, you will see twelve distinct verses in the Bible that use the phrase "good man." These twelve verses detail the standard that God has set for determining a good man. God has given us the answer to all we need to be obedient and successful on this earth.

It is only with God's knowledge and wisdom that we can really identify a good man. Without God's mind and wisdom, our lives become riddled with errors and mistakes. Relationship mistakes have lasting, sometime lifelong consequences. We must have the wisdom of God in that area.

If you are a man reading this you ought to ask yourself, "Am I a good man?" Sometimes we as men compare ourselves to the wrong people. We say, "Well, at least I am not a terrorist," or "I'm not as bad as that guy." We should never compare ourselves to anyone. God's word is the standard. Frankly, none of us measure up to God's standard in our own strength. We all need God's grace and mercy. So even if a man has failed in life, failed God, and failed everyone else depending on him, he can still repent, recover, and be restored to God's standard of a good man.

As you delve into the pages of this book the foundation will be laid in the opening chapters. We will then construct a good man chapter by chapter unveiling each verse in the Bible using the phrase "good man." Once done, we will have finally completed God's standard for a good man.

Chapter 1

Before we confront the standard for a good man, we will examine the claim boldly made by many women that they are a "good woman." The fact is there is not one verse in the Bible from Genesis to Revelation that calls a woman "good." We see women of good understanding, women doing good deeds, but no verse or phrase in the Bible refers to a woman as a "good woman." The Bible describes a woman as virtuous when she is pleasing to God and asks the question, "Who can find a virtuous wife?" Virtuous means possessing moral excellence, uprightness, strength and might. The word virtuous is also translated "army," "valiant," and "man of valor" in the Bible. It is a word of great honor and distinction.

After being in the ministry for nearly 25 years, I have clearly seen why the Bible says, "Who can find a virtuous wife?" There are certain character traits that are attached to that title "virtuous wife." Notice the Bible did not say who can find a Christian wife or godly wife. It says a "virtuous wife." The Hebrew word for "wife" here is the same word translated "woman" as well; so, either word is appropriate here. Whether a woman is single or married this verse applies to her.

Throughout my years of ministry, I have seen men and women who want the best but refuse to be the best. Many women want a good man but don't want to be good for that man. Many men want a virtuous woman but will not meet the standard to have her. It's just as difficult for a man to find a virtuous woman as it is for a woman to identify a good man. The seeming abundance of available single women does not equate to an abundance of virtuous women. A virtuous woman is recognized and celebrated for her uniqueness, not her sameness. Every good man desires a virtuous woman because only a virtuous woman meets the high standards of a good man.

Thank God I have found a virtuous wife. Every good man desires a virtuous woman, but not all of them have found one. A great preacher once declared to me, "You and your father have found good wives. Some of us did not get that." The Bible says, "He who finds a wife finds a good thing." One reason I believe many of God's daughters feel it is so difficult to find a good man is because they are the ones looking. The Bible teaches that women ought to be found by a good man. A woman trying to find a good man is like a dog chasing after its tail, always chasing and never catching. If caught, it brings nothing but pain.

The man should be doing the seeking and he should be the one finding, not the other way around. If you are a single woman you must be able to identify a good man, not find him. Virtuous women have become a rare commodity. So, when a good man finds a virtuous woman he finds her hard to resist. When a woman attains the irresistible characteristics of a virtuous woman, a good man will automatically be drawn to her allowing him to find his "good thing."

Adam and Eve were the first human beings on this earth. God formed man from the dust of the ground personally crafting man himself. Out of Adam's rib He "made" a woman. The Hebrew word for "made" in that verse means "built." Adam was formed, but Eve was "built," giving us the basis for the slang phrase "she's a brick house." Adam and Eve were both created perfect yet they became the greatest failures in the Bible. They had it all and still ate the fruit that was forbidden. God told Adam specifically that he could eat from every tree in the garden except for the tree that was in the middle of the garden. Eve had not yet been created when that command was given to Adam. There is no record that God ever said it again. Therefore, it is apparent that Adam must have communicated the command to his wife. Because of this, Adam was principally responsible for what happened in the garden of Eden.

Eve's initial failure was that she continued to listen to the serpent after he questioned what God said. She should have cut off communication the first instant the serpent questioned God. She would not have been deceived if she had stopped listening. The smooth, appealing words of the serpent captivated Eve and she did not turn away. Deception is only possible by giving ear to a lie. When the serpent was deceiving Eve, it is easy to assume that Adam was somewhere else, doing something else, and Eve found him to give him the forbidden fruit. This, however, was not the case. The Bible says Adam was with her. He apparently was close by and witnessed everything that was taking place.

The Bible says that Adam was not deceived. This means that he was not tricked and he was not fooled. He knew the serpent was lying and he said nothing. Adam also knew his wife believed the lies of the serpent and again he said nothing. He also knew God's commandment and he said nothing. He knew the consequences of disobeying God's commandment and he said nothing. God had given Adam authority over the entire earth at the time and he said nothing. It was the silence of Adam more than the deception of Eve that caused the downfall of man. It is still the appalling silence of men that allows the curse of lying and deception to ruin families, churches, communities, and nations.

After Adam ate the forbidden fruit, the Bible says the eyes of both of them were opened. Because the command not to eat from the tree of the knowledge of good and evil was given to Adam, I don't believe the human race was doomed to sin until he ate of the fruit. The nature of this encounter still happens today. This weak, spineless, rebellious, pathetic excuse for authority still resides in men who will not be strong and become good men. This simple, naive, lie-believing woman is still evident in women who refuse to be virtuous.

The sad thing is neither Adam nor Eve ever repented for their sin. They never went to God or each other and said, "I'm sorry, forgive me. I was wrong." This unrepentant trait in men and women has not changed.

Neither is ever quick to admit when he or she is wrong. Not only did Adam and Eve not repent, they blamed someone else for their failure. Adam blamed Eve and Eve blamed the serpent.

There is also no record of them possessing or owning anything after the fall. They no longer walked in God's blessing. I don't believe this is just because they fell. I believe it's because they never repented. Not only that, but they both hid from God and were uncomfortable in God's presence after the fall. This is why many men and women today are uncomfortable in God's presence. They are uncomfortable with holiness and truth. It is the same nature Adam and Eve had after the fall. There is no record that they ever spoke to God again or had fellowship with Him again. The last thing the Bible records either of them said to God was an excuse for their disobedience.

Adam and Eve are never commended for accomplishing anything in the Bible. The Bible never says, "Be like Adam," or "Be like Eve." This is because of their lack of repentance and fellowship with God. They both lived hundreds of years on a cursed earth and without God's blessing. I believe that if Adam and Eve had repented that they would have been forgiven and allowed to walk in the blessings of God. Sin would still be in the earth, but they could have been great and blessed in their lives.

Adam and Eve are the originators of stubbornness because of their refusal to repent after hundreds of years away from God. Unfortunately, the descendants of Adam and Eve are still trying to come together today and have the same issues as the original Adam and Eve. Sadly, countless men and women don't even see these issues because error and perversity have become normal. Without the light of truth, no one knows what normal should be. No virtuous woman would ever want Adam and no good man would ever want Eve.

Abraham and Sarah are the godly, biblical standard for a husband and wife. Both of them served the Lord with all their heart. They both trusted God and obeyed God which allowed them to walk in His promises and blessing. As a result of God's blessing, they were very wealthy having land, money, cattle, and servants. The greatness of God's blessing, however, was not their wealth, but the significance of their descendants, the nation of Israel, from whom came all eternal truth and the greatest gift to man,

Jesus Christ. This is their enduring legacy. The Bible says that if we are in Christ, we are also Abraham's children.

Once one is in Christ, his heritage and destiny change from Adam and Eve to Abraham and Sarah. He still, however, must learn the right way, choose the right way, and live the right way. If a person commits his life to Christ, he destroys for good the curse of Adam and Eve in his life. Good men are not like Adam but like Abraham and want to be with a woman like Sarah. Virtuous women are not like Eve but like Sarah and will be drawn to men like Abraham. The Bible says that women who do well are daughters of Sarah not daughters of Eve. Sarah influenced Abraham to do God's will. Eve influenced Adam to fall. Eve gave her man the fruit of rebellion and disobedience. Sarah, on the other hand, helped her man fulfill the Lord's call and encouraged his faith and obedience.

Another honorable trait of Sarah is that she knew how to talk to Abraham, which is most important. Sarah spoke to Abraham and treated him with the utmost respect. It is so important that women learn how to talk to men. It is one of the golden keys that make a woman virtuous. This does not mean that she should call her man lord as Sarah called Abraham; but she must understand the power that respect has with men. There are many times when a man may not deserve respect by his life and behavior. In these cases, it is extremely difficult for any woman to show respect to her husband, father, brother, or friend when he has disrespected her or his life and behavior are not deserving of respect. However, it is better to be silent than cross the line of disrespect with words. Even good men are not always so good.

Men remember the words a woman says to him in times of disagreement more than her words to him in times of peace. He will either remember her for her words of wisdom and honor or for her words of insult and disrespect. One pastor said it this way, "You are remembered for either the problems you solve or the ones you create." A virtuous woman should make herself unforgettable by the wisdom of her words in times of stress, not the foolishness of them.

Wisdom with words is something a woman has to learn from a mature, virtuous woman. Often a less mature woman does not realize how poisonous and destructive her words can be. Sometimes this must be revealed to her by another. Once it is known, she must resolve to "learn to do well" if she is going to attract and keep a good man. Her beauty may attract him, but her wisdom will keep him.

Some women make the argument that they are not going to stroke a man's ego. This is a grave mistake. Most men have a great ego. If a man feels good about himself when he's with a woman, he will want to be in her presence as often as possible. No good man will remain in the presence of a woman who makes him feel less than a man, whether he deserves it or not.

Sarah's ability to encourage her man to fulfill God's call, speak to her man with respect, and stand strong in faith herself are master keys as to why Sarah is the biblical standard for a godly wife and woman of God. Learning how to speak to a man is an especially critical trait for a woman to possess in becoming a virtuous woman and retaining a good man. Remember, a virtuous woman must be able to identify a good man and then she will know when she has been found by him.

Chapter 2

Far too often women have bought into lies, fables, and superstitions. Often these lies and fables are old wives tales that have been passed from one generation to the next. For example, the idea that it is bad luck to allow a black cat to cross your path or it is seven years of bad luck if you break a mirror. The list of silly superstitions goes on and on.

Many continue to live their daily lives believing these fables and superstitions. Some people never admit to believing any of these fables or superstitions. However, the evidence a lie has been believed is the behavior that follows. If people avoid black cats, they believe the superstition that it is bad luck. Regardless of what a person says, his corresponding behavior proves his belief in the lie or validates his belief in the truth. There are always consequences to believing a lie and always rewards for believing the truth. The following are some common lies women believe.

Lie #1. A good man will love me for who I am.

This statement is often used as a cop out for a lack of self-improvement and an excuse not to change. There are some things about us we cannot change. However, there are some things about us we can and should change. Some people have bad attitudes and are nearly impossible to get along with because they are mean, nasty and cruel. Then there are those who are sneaky, sly, deceptive, and manipulative and cannot be trusted. No good man wants a woman with such traits and nor should he. No virtuous woman wants a man with those traits nor should she.

We all have the ability to change negative traits in our character regardless of the legitimacy or reason behind those negative traits. There may have been things that happened in a woman's past that contributed to her negative traits. While the events that occurred whether in childhood or adulthood may not have been her fault, she must choose the path of freedom, not the path of excuse. We have to allow the Spirit of God to purge us of traits that are not like Him. With those qualities we cannot change, we must do our best to work with what we have. Ladies, never use this as a cop out. You can change.

<u>Lie #2. The way to a man's heart is through his stomach.</u>

There is no connection between the heart of a man and his stomach. Just cooking for him will not win him. If you do cook for him, please make sure the food is good. Bad cooking will not help your case. Cooking good food for him, however, will promote fond thoughts of you in his mind.

<u>Lie #3. Sleeping with a man will bring us closer together.</u>

Few things are further from the truth than this. There is absolutely no connection between a man's heart and his crotch. This is one of the biggest lies women believe about men. With many men, there is no emotional connection to sex at all. Furthermore, many times there is not even communication between a man's heart and what is between his legs. A man's heart may have no idea what is going on below. Sex creates a strong emotional connection with most women, not with most men. With many men, it is nothing more than a physical release. This is why a man can sleep with a woman and not remember her name or even that he was with her a week later.

There have been a lot of women who have had children in an attempt to keep a man only to end up with multiple children and no man to father them. Untold numbers of young girls have lost their virginity to a man they thought loved them only to find he just played the game. Then there is the continuous lie that because he keeps coming back he must love you. Most of the time it's not love, he just wants some more.

There are countless numbers of women whose lives have been turned upside down because they believed a man loved them. The heart of many women has been broken because they fell for a married man, believing he would leave his wife for her. This is the epitome of foolishness. If a man is already married and can't be trusted to be faithful to his wife, his mistress has no chance. Statistically, only an extremely small percentage of men leave their wives for their mistresses. Even if the man remarries, rarely does he marry the mistress.

While our culture and society accept sexual relations outside of marriage, the word of God does not. When we violate the command of God it only brings heartache, frustration, pain, and drama. Always follow the path of obedience and truth. A good man will want you for what you bring to his life, not just for what you can do for him in the bedroom.

Lie # 4. There are no good men left.

Good men are not common. But, there are many good men. Much of this issue comes from the fantasy that many single women have that a good man is perfect. While women verbally admit there are no perfect men, the standard they set in their own mind and live out with their behavior is one that can only be obtained by God. A good man is not a perfect man. There is also another basis for this untruth as well. Many women base this lie on the limitations of their own experience. They continuously assume that because they don't have a good man, or can't find one, a good man must not exist.

Lie # 5. If he is my man, I can change him.

Most women will quickly deny that they believe this lie. But again, the evidence a lie has been believed is the behavior that follows. Every woman reading this book has the same working parts as other women reading this book. All women who have ever walked the earth have had the same working parts. None of those parts are good enough to change any man. Only by the Spirit of God or some catastrophe will a man change. Some women believe it's her care and affection for a man that will change him. That does not work either. Belief in this lie has caused the pain and emotional ruin of countless women over the years. They falsely believe that they have the power to bring about a permanent change in the man they are with.

The tragedy is while they struggle trying to change a man into what they think he should be, good men come and go and they don't even realize it. One of the biggest dangers is a woman trusting her own strength. The Bible says when we trust in man's strength that we will not see when good comes. This means that the good man a woman dreamed about could be right in front of her but because she trusts in her own strength and not God's, she can't even see him. If a man has to change to be pleasing to God and pleasing to you, you should not be with him.

For a married woman whose husband is not a good man, there is hope. The difference is a single woman goes into a relationship knowing that the man is not pleasing to God. By her decision to do this, she has chosen to eat the fruit of her own way. Her lust for him, her fear of being alone, or the explosive combination of both drive a woman to compromise and accept terms of a relationship without God. She holds on to the baseless hope that God will come to her rescue after she deliberately crossed the line of obedience. God is merciful; but most women who have done this experience years of frustration and pain. Children are often caught in the crossfire and become influenced by a man who refuses to serve the Lord. It's just better to obey God.

A woman who comes to Christ after marrying an unbelieving man walks in a greater degree of grace and favor to bring about change in her marriage because she did not knowingly put herself in that position. If she by wisdom and good character loves this man, God can get his attention. Her love and affection for him authenticate her faith and make it possible for him to listen. This often takes time but God's word promises this can be done for His daughters.

Lie # 6. I'm very busy. A good man will wait for me.

Since a woman is to be found by a good man, her availability is the key. Hurts from previous relationships have caused women to make themselves unavailable, not just for a good man, but for any man. The fear of rejection or being hurt again has plagued them and sent them in the other direction. A good man cannot find his "good thing" if she is unavailable or hiding. Even hard-working, career women have made themselves unavailable. Talking on the phone, going to lunch, dinner, movies, ballgames, or other events are investments for potential long term relationships. When a man is looking for his "good thing," a virtuous woman needs to be in a position to be found. Only God should be her hiding place and He will never put her in a place where she cannot be found.

Lie # 7. I'm grown and I don't need anyone to tell me what to do.

Unless this attitude is corrected and this lie is no longer believed, it will lead to lifelong singleness. In the book of Ruth, Naomi, a mature woman of God, guided Ruth in putting herself in the arena of a man named Boaz. He was not only a godly man, but a good and wealthy man. Naomi was Ruth's mother-in-law. Her husband passed away and she decided to stay with her mother-in-law, who was a virtuous and godly woman, instead of going back to her hometown where her people were pagan and worshiped the devil. Naomi told Ruth what to do, how to do it, and when to do it. Because Ruth listened to Naomi, God allowed her to win the heart of a good man. Once Ruth was in the presence of Boaz, God opened his eyes because she followed the instructions of Naomi. It is interesting to note there are only two women honored with a book in the Bible named after them, Ruth and Esther. Both of them followed the instructions of their mentor to get the man God had ordained for them. Ruth became the great-grandmother of King David, Israel's greatest king, all because she followed the instructions that were given to her. Ruth is one of only four women named in the direct ancestry of Jesus. What an honor!

All lies come from the devil and when believed, even in innocence, bring pain and frustration. Behavior is the real evidence of what is believed. When the truth is known and believed, it will always make you free.

Chapter 3

"So the watchman said, "I think the running of the first is like the running of Ahimaaz the son of Zadok." And the king said, "He is a good man, and comes with good news."

II Samuel 18:27

The first place in the Bible where a man is referred to as a "good man" is in II Samuel 18:27. The man's name was Ahimaaz. His name means "powerful brother." In Bible times the meaning of a person's name reflected the character of that person's life. By knowing a person's name you would know their character. Before we examine the details of this verse some background information is important to understand.

King David was Israel's greatest king. He set the standard for godliness and integrity in a king for all time. Every king after David in the Bible was compared to him. They were either righteous like him or wicked and not like him. David is described as a man after God's own heart. He was a great warrior. When he was just a boy he killed the giant Goliath who was over ten feet tall. As a king, he led the people with the heart of a shepherd. In fact, he was a great shepherd and used by God to write the famous

23rd Psalm that begins with "The Lord is my shepherd." David loved the Lord with all his heart. He praised, worshiped, and danced before the Lord with such passion that once he danced right out of his clothes. God promised that through the line of King David, Jesus, the Savior of the world, would come. There could be no greater honor than that.

King David, however, was not perfect and failed many times. He failed personally, morally, and as a king. Yet the quality that sets David apart from many others is that he quickly and genuinely repented for his sin. Though King David repented for his sins, he was still punished for them. While he was king, he slept with a married woman, Bathsheba. He then had her husband killed to cover it up.

David was still God's anointed king. But, as a result of David's sin, not only did the baby conceived from this sin die, God allowed a rebellion to rise up from within his own house. King David's son, Absalom, rebelled against him and gathered thousands of soldiers in an attempt to overthrow the kingdom. Though God allowed the rebellion, He did not sanction or support it. Absalom's smooth words persuaded enough men to force his father to temporarily flee the capital city of Jerusalem. David was devastated that his own son would rise up against him. In addition to that, David's close friend and top counselor betrayed him and sided with his son. To add insult to injury, Absalom had sex with his father's wives out in public for everyone to see.

This is when Ahimaaz comes on to the scene. When David fled for his life from his son, he left the priest in the city to bring him word on Absalom's plans. The messages were delivered to King David by the priest's sons. Ahimaaz was one of those messengers. Ahimaaz was a man that refreshed the heart of King David during his darkest hours. He risked his life to remain loyal to his king who was discouraged and heartbroken. The word he brought King David spared the king's life and saved the kingdom. Ahimaaz proved his loyalty during the most difficult days of his king's life. His loyalty and trustworthiness stood out in the mind of God's greatest king.

Loyalty and trust are the words that describe Ahimaaz, a "powerful brother." These traits are often lost in our country and culture. Loyalty is a heart allegiance that one expresses towards another. Loyalty breeds trust and trust is one of the most powerful words in our language. One great man of God declares, "It is better to be trusted than to be loved." Love is proof of someone's kindly affection toward another. But trust is proof of a person's godly character. A lot of men in our time claim to be powerful, but there is no doubt that Ahimaaz was truly a "powerful brother."

The verse opens with King David awaiting word on the outcome of the battle to put away the rebellion. When King David sees Ahimaaz running towards him, he comments that he is a "good man." He no doubt remembers the comfort this man's loyalty brought him during his greatest pain. For Ahimaaz to earn the title "good man" from the greatest king anointed by God is a high benchmark for any man to achieve.

Loyalty is a trait that nearly everyone respects, but only a few exemplify. We are consumers by nature. Our free market society has taught us to only be loyal to a person if he has the best deal or serves us better at the moment. Therefore, we are often only loyal to the degree that we personally benefit. Even in the workplace, employers rarely honor employees' years of sacrificial service. They will fire them or lay them off if the company goes through hard times. Similarly, employees are rarely loyal to a company which refused to lay them off during tough times. They disregard the company's sacrifice to keep them and take their talents to the highest bidder.

Even in a church, among those who are supposed to be God's people, loyalty is hard to find. Some churches refuse to recognize, reward, or protect a person who has been dedicated for years. On the other hand, a pastor may have sacrificed his time and energy to help someone out of a crisis, pray tirelessly for him, and help him and his family to know God only to see him leave and go somewhere else for frivolous reasons, taking with him his time, talent, and money. He commits his time, talent, and money to another pastor who has made no investment in his life. God is not pleased with either case. Loyalty is indeed rare. Sometimes it is difficult to determine whether someone is loyal or just faithful to a duty. Someone could be faithful to a duty without being loyal to a person or cause. They could just be faithful for a paycheck or some other benefit. Tough times are the proving grounds for loyalty.

Ahimaaz risked his life because of his loyalty to King David. It would have been easier for him to just go with the flow or go with whoever seemed to be winning at the moment. The root of integrity in him would allow nothing less than loyalty and trust. Because of the multiple betrayals, there is no doubt King David placed great value on those who proved loyal to him. Betrayal by those who are close is the cost of leadership. Nearly every leader has paid that price. Just as there are many that betray their leader, God preserves those who are loyal. Every leader places great value on loyalty. This is a trait that reflects God-like character. Trust is the rock solid trait that is born from proven loyalty.

The matchless traits that Ahimaaz demonstrated were loyalty and trust. They are two traits that will forever be the requirements of a good man. They can be seen in how a man is loyal to those close to him or those who have been good to him. That track record translates into loyalty to the woman he loves. If he is not loyal, then he will likely not be loyal to anyone. These two traits are the foundation for God's standard of a good man. No man can claim the title "good man" without them. Loyalty and trust are the irreplaceable qualities that are woven into the fabric of every good man.

Chapter 4

"The steps of a good man are ordered by the LORD, And He delights in his way."

Psalm 37:23

In the first paragraph of this book, I recalled the U.S. Marines repeated request for "a few good men." Military life is much different than civilian life. Every recruit for the military goes through several weeks of basic training. In the Army, after basic training recruits are transformed from a civilian into a soldier. They are put through rigorous physical, mental, and emotional stressors until their will is finally broken. They arrive doing their own will, but after basic training they won't take a step until they are told.

One of the most important things recruits learn from basic training is how to follow orders. Military men don't do what they want like civilians do; they do what they are ordered to do. As a matter of fact, the first thing that a soldier receives after basic training is his orders. He is told where he is going to serve. The military understands that in combat the lives of all those in battle depend upon soldiers following orders, not instincts. A soldier who will not follow orders cannot be trusted. This is why every man's will in the unit must be broken before the first bullet is ever fired at them.

Whenever we see a military man serving anywhere, we know he is serving there because he was ordered to be there. No soldier goes where he wants; he goes where he is ordered. The superior officer places him there on purpose to perform a certain job. His paycheck, provisions, and all his supplies are at the place he was ordered to go. He is part of a larger plan with many soldiers working together all of whom are following orders. The ability to unequivocally follow orders is the major distinction between a military man and a civilian man.

This passage begins by declaring that the steps of a good man are ordered by the Lord. This is a man who like a military man does not take a step unless he is ordered by God. This does not mean that he cannot think for himself, but that he is no longer his own man. He no longer does his own will, but the will of the one ordering his steps.

Every step of a good man is secure because it was ordered by God. This is like the military man whose ability to follow orders saves his life and the lives of those around him. The good man's ordered steps secure his life and those connected to him. In the combat of life, a good man follows orders not his instincts. Just like a soldier in battle, a man who will not follow orders cannot be trusted in the combat of life. A good man, because he follows orders, brings great security and reassurance in a woman's life. She knows that when things get tough, he will follow orders not instincts. She can then be confident that he won't bail out on her in time of trouble. So, when we see a good man in a certain place, we know he is there because he was ordered not because he ran from somewhere else.

The ability and the will to follow God's orders are some of the most obvious traits of a good man. It is interesting to note that the Bible did not say the steps of a good man are requested by the Lord; they are ordered. God does not give recommendations or suggestions. What God delivers to a man is not multiple choice. The Bible does not give us the ten suggestions. We have the Ten Commandments. We have **the** way, not a way. We have **the** truth, not a truth. One of the clearest ways to identify a good man is to observe if his steps are in line with God's orders.

There are different levels of rank in the military. Each soldier must follow orders from each level of authority above him. A good man is a man who follows God's orders, as well as those orders which come through human authority on earth. It is a fact that God does and always has spoken through His servants. A good man is a man who understands God-given authority in the earth and obeys it.

Because we live in a generation where many men did not have fathers in their lives growing up, there is often a void in them. Many have a difficult time understanding authority. A father provides that authority and discipline that every young man desperately needs. When God created the earth, He created a garden to put man in. He would not allow anything to grow until a man was there to till the ground. God did not place man in a forest; He placed him in a garden. In a forest, there is wild and unrestrained growth. In a garden, everything grows on purpose. Flowers are pruned and grow where and how they are planted. In a forest, weeds grow with no purpose, plan, or pruning. This is what happens to a man without a father or spiritual father to discipline him. He becomes like a weed in the earth, wild and unrestrained, not producing in his life the beautiful garden God intended. Even if a man did not have a father in his life, if he chooses to follow God's orders, the Lord will reserve for him a spiritual father so nothing in his life goes lacking. This applies to a woman who did not have a father as well.

When a father is in a boy's life, he gives his son the image of what a man should be. The young man sees the image of a godly man to imitate so he too can be a good man. Far too often what a young man sees growing up is a man who refuses to serve the Lord. Sometimes he sees a man who mistreats women, is proud, cocky, uncommitted, and not submitted to anyone. This young man then grows up copying the behavior of a man who is not worth imitating. It is important to remember that a young man cannot imitate what he does not see; but what he sees he will ultimately imitate.

The tragedy is that some men want to be in authority but are not under authority. When a person is in authority but is not under authority it always produces a mess. I have told single women over the years that the man she is seeing should have a man in his life that can correct him and tell him he is wrong. Not just that, he needs to actually listen to that man. I have told these women if their man does not have a person of authority in his life or there is no one he will listen to, run for your lives! If there is no authority in his life then he is uncovered, unadvised, uncounseled, and uncorrected. If he remains in that condition, there is nothing but disaster down that path.

The verse concludes with God delighting in the way of a good man. This is because the good man chose to follow God's orders. His steps are secure and his path is clear and straight. His life has purpose and meaning because he abides in the master plan of God. The future of a good man is sure because God always pays for what he orders. A good man is a man who is under authority and follows orders. God is pleased with his way.

Chapter 5

Nearly every movie that is labeled an action movie has a male star who is loaded with testosterone. He is a man's man in every sense of the word. He is strong, manly, and he doesn't take junk from anyone. He's portrayed as having good ethics but with a strong stubborn streak as well. At the end of the movie, he always gets the girl.

It's good to show men who are strong and manly. In our society, we have seen the lines between masculinity and femininity blurred in recent years. Make no mistake; God gave men testosterone for a reason. That's what makes a man a man. Men are supposed to be physically stronger, have deeper voices, and not be as emotional or as sensitive as women. It's normal for men to be competitive, a little rough, and beat their chest (so to speak) when they win. He made men to be driven to succeed and accomplish goals. Testosterone was no accident God designed us this way.

Unfortunately, in our time and culture, manhood is not celebrated. There seems to be a drive in this country, by some, for the feminization of men. For some reason, they are trying to make our men more like women. This is a contributing factor as to why large numbers of men in our country don't like going to church. They see church as somewhere women go for an emotional release. They don't see the relevance to them. In addition to that, the church tends to cater to its main constituency, which is women.

When it comes to church, it seems that the only thing men hear about manhood is how to be a good husband or how to be a good father. They are taught this from the slant of what the women want the men to do. Yes, we as men should be good husbands and fathers. However, there is more to being a good man than just being a good husband and father. Rarely do men hear that it is alright to think like a man, act like a man, and be a man. Men need to know it's godly to be a real man.

Even the images we see of Jesus seem to portray feminine characteristics. In an effort to show the humility and meekness of Jesus in a work of art, He is often shown with rosy cheeks and the appearance of wearing lipstick and make-up. He often appears soft and not manly. A careful study of the Bible, however, reveals a very different picture of our Lord. The Bible says His earthly father Joseph was a carpenter. Jesus would have been trained in this trade as a child. Imagine having to make furniture or other items of wood without the use of power tools. Everything had to be carved and chiseled by hand. Picking up heavy pieces of wood day in and day out would naturally build strength, which means He likely had very strong arms.

We hear the description of Jesus being as gentle as a lamb. This is true. But I am reminded of the time Jesus went into the temple while people were buying and selling. Not only was there buying and selling, but corruption as well. After seeing this corruption, Jesus was angered, pulled out a whip, and drove out all those who bought and sold in the temple. He also turned over the tables and the seats of those who sold. Picture this: people are making money and He comes in and turns over their tables, knocking all their money and goods on the floor. It is likely the men were still sitting in those seats when Jesus turned them over because no one just gets up and leaves money on the table. Can you imagine Jesus doing all this and nobody said a word? I don't believe their silence was just due to their respect for God. I believe they probably saw his facial expression and strong arms then decided it was in their best interest to be quiet.

The idea we hear often that Jesus was somehow politically correct is also grossly untrue and not biblically accurate. While it is true that Jesus' preaching and teaching was with love and compassion, He was still extremely bold and confrontational. The religious establishments of His day were routinely offended. This was not because He intended to offend them but because their hearts were cold, callous, and unrepentant. They hated the truth because it disrupted the power and influence they enjoyed. Jesus, while on earth, was the personification of love, truth, grace, and mercy. Yet, He was a real man. The manhood of Jesus is proof that a man can be loving, merciful, and gracious without losing his testosterone-laden manhood.

There is a story in the Bible where a woman was brought to Jesus who was caught in the very act of adultery. During this time in Israel, adultery carried the death sentence. The religious leaders brought her to Jesus and asked if she should be stoned. They in their hypocrisy reminded Him of what the law said. It is interesting that they only brought the woman to Him, not the man. It does take two to commit adultery. In addition to that, in order to catch her in the very act, they had to know where to find her and be watching her. The question must be asked, how did they know where to find her and as religious leaders why were they watching her? Without contradicting the law Jesus told them, "He who is without sin among you, let him throw a stone at her first." Being convicted, they all went away one by one. When all of them had departed Jesus asked the woman, "Where are those accusers of yours? Has no one condemned you?" She responded, "No one, Lord." Then, Jesus in grace and mercy says to her, "Neither do I condemn you, go and sin no more."

The verse for this chapter opens by saying, "A good man deals graciously." Gracious is not a word that would normally be used to describe a man. But seeing how Jesus could be both manly and gracious means the two words can exist together. The word "gracious" is also rendered "show favor." This is a man who shows mercy, has pity, and is considerate.

The downside to the action movie hero, manly man image is that another trait often associated with it is stubbornness. This hard, difficult to deal with, unwilling to yield or comply type of man is seldom gracious and nearly impossible to live with. We, as men, cannot be this way if we are to have the honor of being a good man. The unfortunate reality, however, is that stubbornness plagues large numbers of men. We all struggle with it sometimes.

I remember one occasion when my wife and I made a profit from a real estate transaction. We still had repairs to complete on another property, but I wanted a king size bed and everything that came with it. I'm a very tall man, so I justified my desire for a king size bed. I also wanted a 65" high definition TV for our family room. I worked hard on these real estate deals and I wanted to see some tangible reward. My wife on the other hand objected, pointing out that we had other obligations to pay first. I was upset and felt that I deserved this reward. She ultimately yielded because of my insistence.

As it turned out, we spent several thousand dollars on the TV and stereo equipment to go along with it. We also bought the king size bed and bedroom furniture. However, we needed that money to complete the other renovations. The result of me not bending and getting the TV and furniture was we ended up having to borrow money to complete the renovations. My stubbornness got us into debt which was nothing short of a headache for years.

Stubbornness is associated with idolatry in the Bible. It is one of those sins that is hard for a person to see. Rarely do we want to equate our character traits with sin when in actuality some of our character traits are sin. I just had to have that TV and king size bed and my justification for having it became my idol for the moment. The comparing of stubbornness to idolatry reveals the serious and wicked nature of this sin. A good man, while still a real man, must overcome stubbornness and deal graciously.

A good man is also a giver. The Bible says in this verse that, "A good man deals graciously and lends." Giving is a characteristic that is very much like God. Our God is a giver. In fact, He is the giver of everything good and perfect. Stinginess and refusal to give are unlike God. All sin is born from selfishness and self-centeredness. The devil is the author of them both. Everything becomes about what I think, what I feel, and what I want.

Just as we discussed earlier, King David had to have Bathsheba, who happened to be another man's wife. He didn't consider anything else but his own lust. David committed adultery and took an innocent man's life to satisfy his own desires. Bathsheba wasn't innocent in this drama either. She purposely bathed herself outside, in plain sight of the king's palace, and didn't protest or resist when King David sent for her. The lure of being with a handsome, rich, and powerful king trumped the commitment Bathsheba had to her husband. As we mentioned in chapter three, it cost both of them dearly.

When love is present, on the other hand, the first thing it wants to do is give. Selfishness takes and hoards; love gives. A good man is a giving man. The greatest evidence that a man loves a woman, even before he says it, is his willingness to protect her and give to her. He doesn't just protect her physically, but he protects her name and reputation. He makes sure she is not put in a dangerous or difficult situation. He watches how she dresses, knowing how men think. When he gives to her, it's not just money or things. But he gives to her the most precious thing he has, his time. His willingness to share meaningful people, places, and things proves that he trusts her.

Love's first instinct is to give. A woman should never deny a man the privilege of protecting her or giving to her as long as he is not trying to buy her. Even if his giving seems annoying to her, he is proving his love and affection for her and she should let him show it. For men love is an action, not a word or emotion. So ladies, never overlook the action, even if he is slow to say those three words you want to hear.

The last phrase in the verse says, "He will guide his affairs with discretion." Discretion is the ability to exercise sound judgment in all areas of life and in all situations. This is the description of a man whose life is under an umbrella of wisdom. A man who guides his affairs with discretion is a man who is protected from needless mistakes and headaches. Discretion makes a man "drama proof." Adversity is something we all must face from time to time but drama is something entirely different. Drama is unnecessary trouble and frustration. One minister says, "Ninety percent of pain in life comes from trusting the wrong people." Discretion guards against trusting, connecting, or associating with the wrong people. It is knowing when to speak, what to speak, or if to speak. Discretion is the ability to keep one's cool in highly emotional occasions when angered, disrespected, or offended. Discretion says and does what is right not what it thinks or feels.

This discretion is not intelligence, education, or book knowledge. It's a component of wisdom that only comes from God. The evidence of discretion is the words from a man's mouth and the quality of a man's decisions, especially during times of difficulty or times of prosperity. Dr. Martin Luther King said, "The ultimate measure of a man is not where he stands in times of comfort and convenience, but where he stands in times of challenge and controversy."

A good man deals graciously, gives, and guides his affairs with discretion. God gave men testosterone to make men different from women. That difference should be celebrated not apologized for. Jesus was a real man yet the ultimate example of graciousness and discretion. These are powerful elements in the building of a good man.

Chapter 6

"A good man obtains favor from the LORD, But a man of wicked intentions He will condemn."

Proverbs 12:2

There are many verses in Proverbs which contrast righteousness and wickedness. They reveal how much it matters to God how we live. Our conduct and behavior are important to Him. Through those and other passages we see God respond to certain behaviors of people positively all the time and certain behaviors negatively all the time. He is very predictable.

The common cliché that, "The Lord works in mysterious ways," is neither biblical nor true. God's response to man is very predictable. He is not schizophrenic or moody. Our days, weeks, months, and years are proof of His predictable nature. On the other hand, because the Lord is sovereign and omnipotent, the various ways He brings His promises to pass are unimaginable. No matter how hard we try to analyze things in life, we have to conclude that He is just God. His ways may not be our ways, but His responses are predictable.

Obedience, faith and worship are the three guaranteed ways to get a positive response from God. The desperate step of faith impresses Him. Jesus always responded positively to those who disregarded their own dignity and reputation and reached out to Him in faith. He always responded positively to those who took incredible risks to touch Him and be touched by Him. Favor and blessings were the natural results.

There was a friend of mine that got caught up in a legal situation some years ago. Though he was not a criminal and had committed no crime, his unwise business associations got him into legal trouble. His company's assets put him in a position where he did not qualify for public legal aid. Those assets, however, were tied up through this wrong association; so, he had no financial means to secure an attorney. He sat in the courtroom waiting to be called, knowing he faced potential jail time. In desperate straits, this servant of the Lord cried out to God.

Just as his name was called an unknown man walked into the courtroom and told the judge he represented my friend. The unknown gentleman then asked the judge for a moment of consultation with his client. In the consultation room, this attorney gave my friend instructions on what to do when they went back in to face the judge. My friend in shock asked, "Who are you?" The man replied, "Never mind who I am. Just follow these instructions." He continued to question the attorney about who he was and who sent him, but with no reply.

When they re-entered the courtroom and faced the judge, my friend followed the instructions that were given to him. Immediately the charges were dropped and the record expunged! The attorney walked out of the courtroom and was never seen again! God still uses angels to protect and bless his people who need favor. This reminds me of the famous part of a preacher's sermon, "He'll be a doctor in the sickroom. He'll be a lawyer in the courtroom!" There is no doubt from this story God will!

Very few people in the Bible had more hardship or were shown more favor than Joseph in the book of Genesis. He was born the youngest son of Jacob. Because Joseph was the son of his old age, Jacob loved Joseph more than his other sons. He gave him gifts that he did not give his other sons. This failure on the part of Jacob caused Joseph's brothers to hate him. Not only that, Joseph being young and naive shared his dreams of greatness with them and they hated him even more. His brothers' hatred ran so deep that they sold him into slavery and told their father he was killed. Joseph was hurt, betrayed, and now enslaved. Because he was a man of God though, his character and integrity were still rock solid even through these devastating events. This proven display of character paved the way for God to give him favor and fulfill his destiny.

The first requirement to obtain favor is to be pleasing. Joseph pleased God by his godly character during his darkest days. Even as a slave, Joseph worked as if he was being paid. This caused those above him to trust him and promote him. Once promoted Joseph ran the house of a very wealthy and prominent Egyptian named Potiphar.

Joseph was a handsome man and very pleasing to the eye. Potiphar's wife tried many times to seduce him but he refused. In her desperation to get him, she grabbed him and would not let him go. Joseph's obedience to God and loyalty to Potiphar would not let him yield. He ran out of the house leaving his clothes in her hands. Potiphar's wife in anger lied on Joseph. She accused him of raping her, and had him thrown into prison. Even in prison Joseph received favor for his character and integrity. He was trusted to be in charge even in prison.

Joseph as a man of God could interpret dreams. While in prison, he accurately interpreted a fellow prisoner's dream that he would get out and serve the king. This man forgot Joseph when he got out until Pharaoh, King of Egypt, had a dream that no one could interpret. Joseph was called in and accurately interpreted the king's dream. He was miraculously promoted to second in command behind only the king himself and had authority over the most powerful country in the world at the time!

Because of God's favor, Joseph went from being a prisoner to Prime Minister in less than 24 hours! His brothers who hated him and sold him into slavery had to come to him for food for their families. Joseph could have had them killed or let them starve to death. Instead, he showed them mercy and restored them in family unity.

Several years ago I knew someone who went to prison for a crime he did not commit. He was a police officer accused of using his position to help family and friends break the law without being caught. His trial was viewed by some as a political opportunity to demonstrate toughness. Though he was acquitted of all felony charges, they still sent him to jail. He was devastated.

While he was in prison his wife never went to see him, never wrote, or communicated with him at all. She completely abandoned him during the time of his greatest need. In addition to that, she never brought his children to see him and would not even let them write him a letter. For nearly five years he did not see or even hear from his wife and kids. He was broken beyond words. To make matters worse, he was placed in the general population in prison. Since he was a former police officer, this was not supposed to be done. It was very dangerous for him because he had put some of those same prisoners behind bars. His life was literally in danger constantly. He lost everything and nearly gave up thinking his life was over.

During those years I encouraged him and constantly reminded him that his life was not over and God had a great plan for him. He continued to seek the Lord and served as assistant chaplain in the prison. He was also used to speak to troubled young men to encourage them and set them on the right path. Despite this, he was still repeatedly turned down for parole while hardened criminals were set free. In my meetings with him prior to his release, I told him that if he was faithful to God, his release would be the beginning of his life not the end.

After five years of mental and emotional hell, he was finally released. God began to move quickly on his behalf. He listened to counsel, followed instructions, and was faithful to God and the church. Within a month of his release he found a job and was promoted to manager. A few months later, he was voted manager of the year after working with the company only six months.

This man, determined to get his life back on track, served God with all of his might. While serving the Lord, a beautiful woman of God caught his eye. She had been faithful for years. She was consistently in church, active, and listened to the counsel given to her. As a quiet woman, she never created any trouble or caused her pastor any grief. She was and still is a joy to her pastor. So, the fact that she got a good man was no accident.

Every single woman should follow her example. They should be faithful, committed, and obedient. Then, God can trust them with one of his best sons. After they met, they both followed careful instructions and went through months of counseling. After the completion of counseling they were married. Within one year of his release, God restored his children back to him, gave him a great career, and blessed him with a virtuous woman with whom to spend his life! A good man truly obtains favor! With God on the throne and breath in our bodies, there is always hope!

This verse says a good man obtains favor from the Lord. Since the first requirement of favor is to be pleasing, a good man must be pleasing to God to obtain favor. Favor is good will, delight, and acceptance. When a person is shown favor they are advanced, promoted, prospered, and blessed. They move to the front of the line when they were in the back of the line. They get hired when they were less qualified for the job than others. Someone delighted in them and showed them favor. Favor is not favoritism. Favoritism is unjust partiality, but favor is no accident. It is a just reward for a life of obedience and faith. Favor may be unfair, but is never unjust.

A good man must therefore be a man of faith and integrity as Joseph was. Without faith it is impossible to please God. A good man walks by faith, pleases God, and obtains favor like my friend did. When a man is pleasing to God, favor will be evident in his life.

Chapter 7

"A good man leaves an inheritance to his children's children, But the wealth of the sinner is stored up for the righteous."

Proverbs 13:22

In the 2008 Olympic Games, Usain Bolt broke the world record in the hundred meters with a blazing time of 9.69 seconds. After his record setting performance, he earned the title of the fastest man in the world. As great as this accomplishment was, there were two other men who ran one hundred meters faster than Bolt in the same Olympics. Their hundred meter times of 8.70 seconds and 9.01 seconds where much faster than Bolt's hundred meter sprint. They were the 2nd and 3rd leg of the Jamaican 4x100 meter relay team.

Unlike the 100 meter dash, the 2nd, 3rd, and 4th legs of the 4x100 meter relay do not start in the starting block. With a relay team, all the legs after the 1st leg get a running start before the baton is passed to them. So by the time each of the last three men starts their one hundred meter leg, they are already at a full sprint.

This is what God had in mind when he commanded the fathers to teach their children His ways. By doing this, there is a progression of knowledge that increases with each generation. The current generation should leave the next generation an inheritance. That inheritance should be spiritual and material. In order to leave a spiritual inheritance, God commanded his people to only marry another person of God. He warned that the ungodly spouse would turn their hearts away from Him. Not only that, but He wanted them to raise children that would fear the Lord.

When a person of God marries someone who is not a person of God, there is a conflict as to how their children are raised and what they are taught. The children are raised in spiritual confusion that carries into their adult lives. God knows that a child raised to serve Him will be an adult that will always serve Him. The Lord always has the next generation in mind when he is looking at us.

This verse says that, "A good man leaves an inheritance to his children's children." An inheritance is something that is left to you. It is a character trait, a trade, or material possession. When an inheritance is left to someone, he gets something handed down to him without his own effort. He gets it, but he didn't work for it. The inheritance is something that he has but didn't earn. The person receiving an inheritance gets character traits, a trade, or wealth when he didn't work for it, didn't earn it, and may not have deserved it. He became the beneficiary of the work, labor, and effort of another. The key for one obtaining an inheritance is the relationship between the one giving the inheritance and the one receiving it being right. Broken or strained relationships cut off the pipeline of the inheritance blessing. The one receiving the inheritance should make sure the relationship stays intact.

Maintaining life insurance is one way for a man to leave an inheritance of wealth to his children. But, he must make sure his children are taught well so they can handle what is left to them. Many years ago I was a financial wreck. Not only that, but I mismanaged what I did have. I was taught to save money. I was taught to invest money. I was taught to live on a budget and to pay cash for what I needed instead of getting into debt. Yet, I bought several items on credit and had no budget. At this particular point in my career, I made a pretty good salary and had two roommates that were paying me $300 per month each. My house payment at the time was only $428 per month and I had no wife or kids. Yet, to this day, I cannot tell you why

I was broke or where my money went. I was taught better and knew better, yet I still made foolish decisions.

I am the oldest of three children. Despite my being the oldest, my father at the time made my sister the executor of his estate in case something happened to him. She was very disciplined and frugal. No doubt she handled money much better than I did so this made sense because of my foolish behavior and bad decisions, particularly with money. I had not proven by my behavior that I could handle the distribution of a large sum of money. Quite frankly, I couldn't even handle a small sum. He was not going to trust his inheritance to me until I had proven worthy of that honor. If a man leaves an inheritance to a fool, he will squander the money and ruin himself. Thank God I got it together and I am now trusted to be the executor of my father's estate.

With the 4x100 meter relay team, the 2nd, 3rd, and 4th legs benefit from the labor of the previous leg. So when they run their leg, they don't start from scratch. They are already off and running when they start their race. A good man insures that when his race is finished, his children and grandchildren are already running when he passes them the baton. He has prepared for their success while he was running his leg. When a man does this, he moves from just being successful to being significant. An individual's success only matters in their lifetime. Significance, however, comes with investment into the lives of others. For there to be real significance, our success must out live us. A good man is not just successful, but significant, because he gives the next two generations a running start.

Every parent leaves their children some inheritance, positive or negative. The reason many adults struggle throughout life is because the only things left to them were bills and bad habits. When a man commits his life to Christ, he begins to leave a legacy of truth to his children. They grow up watching him, imitating him, and being taught by him. God's truth is permanently etched in their hearts. They become forever branded as servants of God, trusted and used by Him generation after generation. Many of you reading this book never got a good spiritual or material inheritance. God is now looking to you to be a generation changer so that all those who come after you will benefit from your labor and good decisions. You, as the generation changer, will also be blessed and prospered by God because it is through you that your descendents will receive their natural and spiritual inheritance.

My grandfather, Dr. Waymond L. Burton Sr., was born one of eleven children in the early 1920's. His other siblings dropped out of school to go work in the mill. But for some reason, he was unable to get a job. Therefore, he continued and graduated from high school. He was offered the opportunity to go to college on a singing scholarship. (I have wondered about this for years because neither I nor my father can sing a lick!) He accepted the scholarship and finished college. My grandfather was the only one of eleven children to earn a college degree. During this time he had a neighbor that he would not let out do him in anything. (This is the only situation where it is good to keep up with and pass the "Joneses.") When his neighbor got a masters degree, he said, "I'm smarter than him, if he can get a masters degree so can I." So he went and got his masters degree. The final one-upmanship was my grandfather earning his doctor's degree.

As a result of his efforts, a legacy of education was passed down. All five of his children have college degrees of which my father is one. All of his grandchildren, which includes me as the oldest, have college degrees as well. Only one child of his other 10 siblings got a college degree. While this does not mean they were not successful, my grandfather's legacy of education passed down to us and opened big doors. This is the type of legacy God intends a good man to leave, not necessarily education, but a spiritual legacy of service to God. He also wants us to leave a financial legacy of abundance and prosperity as well as a legacy of good character and honor. A man does this through his own commitment to God first then through life insurance, savings, investments, and businesses. He not only exemplifies these spiritual and practical principles, but also teaches them to his children.

There is an automobile commercial that asks the question, "How long will you be remembered, by whom and for what?" These are questions every man must ask himself and every woman must ask about the man she is with or aspires to be with. The correct answers to those questions provide the path to significance. My wife's great grandfather Charlie Spivey left his children over one hundred acres of land. To this day, many of her relatives still live on that land. A portion of this land with a house on it will be willed to my wife. This she will pass to our children. Charlie Spivey will be remembered by his children for at least four generations.

The good man looks ahead to the 2nd, 3rd, and 4th legs of his family race. He makes sure that they all have a running start. He is remembered for generations by his children and grandchildren because he passed the baton to them at a full sprint in life. He leaves them a spiritual and financial inheritance which will never be forgotten.

Chapter 8

"The backslider in heart will be filled with his own ways, But a good man will be satisfied from above."

Proverbs 14:14

I have been playing golf for many years now. The equipment that a golfer uses is very important. There are certain types of irons in the golf world called "forged" irons. This means that they were made from one piece of soft metal. Being made from one piece of metal instead of two or more pieces put together gives the clubs better quality and consistency. Using a softer metal gives the clubs a more comfortable feel and makes them easier to handle.

Character is the same way. God forges us into shape. This is more difficult than just welding two separate pieces together but worth it. He wants us to be a soft metal, adjustable and bendable, easily yielding to the form of the master's design. When we are "forged" there are no cracks and seams. Our integrity is consistent and solid throughout.

In this verse, we again see a contrast between two different types of men. The ability to distinguish a man with good character from a man whose character is littered with holes and cracks is most valuable, particularly for a woman. It is puzzling that even the most spiritually committed, highly intelligent women somehow still seem to connect with men who were literally just pieced together. The frequency by which this occurs is an indication that spiritual maturity and intelligence are not enough. These traits must be combined with wisdom and counsel.

A woman must have, however, the willingness to listen and follow counsel. I emphasize listen and follow. This is because so many women mistakenly believe that their intelligence and spirituality exempt them from making foolish decisions. They often conclude that they are grown and know what to do; so, counsel and advice are fine but not for them. Just like lie #7 women believe which we discussed in chapter two. Every single woman regardless of her spiritual maturity, knowledge, age, intelligence, or education needs counsel and a team to help her identify a good man. This team consists of her father, her pastor, her mentor, and godly friends. They help her identify a good man and expose the wrong one. We will discuss the details of this team later.

Single women need counsel, not advice. Counsel comes from the authorities in her life and carries much more weight than simple advice. Anyone with an opinion can give advice, but counsel comes from authority. Her father, pastor, and mentor are the main authorities here. God places them in a woman's life as a shield of protection and a light of direction. The difference between counsel and advice is like the difference between making a choice and rendering a decision. Judges have people's lives and future in their hands. They don't make choices; they render decisions. It's the difference between just saying something and speaking with authority. Speaking with authority makes things happen. Obedience to counsel causes her to avoid the tragic mistake of failing to recognize a good man from one who is not.

One minister calls this discerning of character the "Law of Recognition." If a woman cannot discern the man she is with is a fool and she refuses to heed counsel, then she continues in a relationship that is headed for ruin. This verse gives us a key way to recognize rock solid character from one that is hollow and frail. Any character that is hollow cannot maintain its form with the impacts of life. It becomes tattered, cracked, and warped. The impacts of life affect everyone. But, those whose character is solid and forged maintain integrity through them all.

The word backslider is used in this verse. A backslider is someone who slides back, turns back, or moves back from previously held convictions and from serving God. They may deny they don't still have the same convictions; but their lifestyle and behavior no longer uphold them. They look like Michael Jackson when he did the moonwalk, legs moving forward but the body is sliding back. This is the only verse in the Bible that uses the word backslider. The main characteristic of a backslider is their obsession with their own way. Burger King has a slogan that says, "Have it your way." Backsliders do life their own way. Their life is not governed by anything but their own opinion. Their opinion usurps the authority of their righteous convictions and becomes an idol. Any opinion becomes an idol when it begins to trump the truth in a person's life.

The most dangerous man for any woman to date is a man familiar with truth, but not governed by it. He is aware of the boundaries of truth, but refuses to live within them. He is dangerous because his familiarity with truth camouflages his rejection of it. He then becomes the extremely deceptive combination of a lie and truth mixed together. This is much more dangerous than a blatant lie because it is so believable. The lie is often concealed by the smidgen of truth. The small amount of truth may make him appear to be a good man but the mixture with a lie confirms he is not. In the end, truth mixed with anything but truth is a lie.

A man's habitual behavior reveals his nature. Habitual bad behavior is not imperfection but an indication of a character that is hollow and full of cracks. Everyone makes mistakes, but habitual bad behavior is not a mistake. There are many people who play the "I'm not perfect" card to justify bad behavior. They live a life of habitual bad behavior and believe that their claim of imperfection will bail them out of any trouble their behavior got them in. A man or woman like this has no motivation to change because the excuse of imperfection soothes their conscience enough to stay the way they are. While it is true no one is perfect, the key indicator of a person's nature is habitual behavior.

This verse indicates a good man is satisfied from above. The use of the word "satisfied" is key. A man who is not satisfied from above is a man who will try to be satisfied everywhere else. It is worth noting that when God created Adam, He gave him Eve. He did not give him Eve, Susan, Betty, Jane, and Alice. The idea of a man having multiple wives or multiple women is a perversion that was not God's plan. A man named Lamech in the Bible was the first man to have more them one wife. He was an ungodly man and the second murderer on earth. He started a custom of powerful men having multiple women. Jesus put an end to the acceptance of this custom when he declared, "The two shall be one flesh." This perversion however is still prevalent in ungodly men. Even today, it is illegal to have more than one wife, but ungodly men still have more than one woman.

King Solomon was the son of the great King David we discussed earlier. As a king, he had unlimited wealth, unlimited political power, and unchallenged authority. He had no restraint of pleasure and set the standard of wealth and excess for all time. He was the richest man who ever lived. Bill Gates and Warren Buffett could not shake a stick at him. In addition to that, he had 700 wives and 300 concubines! Solomon had 1000 woman at his disposal anytime! He could be with a different woman every night for nearly three years. Some of his wives and concubines might only be with him three times in ten years.

A concubine was more than a modern mistress; she was like a lesser wife. She was legally bound to a man, but did not have all the rights of a full wife. She was often a servant girl that worked for the man of the house and provided sexual services to him. While most men reading this get excited just thinking about it, this proved to be the downfall of King Solomon. God promised that multiplying wives and unrestrained pleasure would bring destruction and it did. Though King David was a great king, his son Solomon saw him with multiple wives and concubines. David did not have as many. But Solomon did what most sons do; they imitate their father's behavior and multiply it in their own life.

There was a time in my life when I was less committed to God than I am now. As a single man during that time I had many women around me who I called "friends." We did things together, however, that were more than just friendly. Calling them friends was a safe place for me to put them so I could sleep with them without making any commitments. I classified all of those women into three groups. The first group of women I would never take anywhere. I considered them unattractive or unqualified to be on my arm. All I did with this group was mess around and lay down. They were like a Playstation; we played with each other but we never left the house. We watched TV and movies, ate popcorn, and slept together, but that was it. There was not a chance of there being anything between us. I was not mean to them nor did I intentionally try to hurt them. I did not lie to them directly, but my motives were a lie.

The second group of women I would at least take out. They were attractive enough to me and carried themselves well enough to be seen with me. We went to movies, dinner, and of course we slept together. They were not, however, what I considered to be marriage potential. This was because they were either ungodly or had some other issue or habit that I did not want in a wife. I was not mean to them nor did I intentionally try to hurt them either. I was caring and compassionate, but at the same time I was selfish and had the wrong motives. There were times I tried to keep an emotional distance so I would not hurt them. But lust being the basis for the relationship made that impossible.

The third group of women I considered to be marriage potential and did not typically sleep with them. They were attractive, godly, and had high standards. I saw them as someone who could help me in my life. I evaluated them based on their attitude, how they spoke to me, and how they responded to me. If they had a bad attitude or were mouthy, I put them in the recycle bin. If they were moody, unreliable, unavailable, or untrustworthy I put them there too. I looked very closely at these women because I considered a possible future with them. I never told any of those women, however, how I evaluated them. Even though in many respects I was thinking with the wrong head, at that point in my life I had enough wisdom not to make a dumb marriage decision. I was similar to my father in this regard when he declared as a single man, "I at least know what I don't want!"

Many women reading this are probably appalled at what I did and how I treated women. Frankly, I am very sorry for the way I behaved myself during those years of my life. I knew better and should have done better. Those women did not deserve to be classified and treated that way. Some of them were great women and I wish I could undo what I did. My heart was tender but my flesh was in control. I was familiar with the truth. In fact, I knew truth well, but I struggled with the boundaries that truth set. I went back and forth over those boundaries hurting myself and others in the process. Ultimately, I did repent for my sinful behavior, asked the Lord to forgive me, and made a decision to obey God's word. Thank God for His forgiveness and His mercy on me!

This is a struggle many men have in becoming a good man. The abundance of women and the lure of pleasure make this struggle difficult for any man. Despite my foolishness, I continued to hear the word of God consistently. This positive habit strengthened me and fed me with wisdom. As I matured spiritually, I began to put away my foolish behavior. My consistency in hearing the word and being active in church was the key. The boundaries of truth are for protection, not bondage.

Solomon had everything that money and power afforded him. Yet, after assessing it all, Solomon said, "All is vanity and grasping for the wind." Pursuit of satisfaction any other way but from above becomes the impossible task of trying to catch the wind. The good man has learned this and is satisfied from above. He knows who he is and is comfortable in his own skin. His self worth is derived from who God made him, not who he made himself. A good man understands that his manhood is not defined by the number of women he sleeps with or the power he has. One woman will never be enough for the man who tries to satisfy himself. A good man knows one woman is more than enough for one man. He understands that lust never satisfies; it always craves more and more is never enough.

The strength a good man receives from God gives him the power to stay within the boundaries of truth. His character is forged and solid. He is a good man and he is satisfied from above.

Chapter 9

"The good man is perished out of the earth: and there is none upright among men: they all lie in wait for blood; they hunt every man his brother with a net."

Micah 7:2 KJV

This verse reflects the view of many single women. They argue that there are no good men left, that all of them have vanished from the earth. The previous verse describes the feeling of being hungry and going into a vineyard expecting to see at least a few good grapes only to find that all of them are taken. In addition to that, there is the painful discovery the few that are left have rotted on the vine. The little known prophet Micah continues and declares there are none upright, they all wait for blood and hunt with a net. These phrases describe the various vices and crimes of the men in the days of Micah. Waiting for bloodshed means those who are lurking to take someone's life. Hunting someone with a net speaks of trapping others with intent to do harm. Nothing has changed. Men today still have the same vices and the same crimes.

As we read this verse, it is very easy to assume the Bible validates the notion of there being no good men left.

This verse, however, records the candid frustrations of a prophet who was discouraged because of the gross ungodliness during his time. He was not documenting facts nor speaking what God was telling him to say at that moment. It's similar to an occasion when the prophet Elijah, in fatigue, frustration, and discouragement complained to God that he was the only one left who served Him. He was running for his life from Jezebel, an evil woman married to a wicked king. Jezebel promised to hunt down Elijah and kill him. The problem with Jezebel was not just her putting on excessive make-up as some have argued. Jezebel had a demon. Make-up can't make anybody that mean! While Elijah was discouraged, God replied to him that He had thousands more godly people. Elijah just did not know about them. He was venting his feelings at that moment, but what he felt was not true.

Elijah was speaking from his limited knowledge. Many people have heard about the cry of Job in the Bible when he lost everything. He uttered the famous words, "The Lord giveth and the Lord taketh away, blessed be the name of the Lord." While his faith was noble, his statement was untrue. God did not take from Job; the devil did. We know this by reading the previous chapter but Job did not know it. He, too, was speaking in anguish from his limited knowledge.

The prophet Micah here is doing the same thing. His feelings at the moment are not true. This can also be said about the feelings of many women who believe there are no good men left. Anyone who assumes all good men are gone or taken is also speaking from limited knowledge. This assumption is the basis for lie # 4 that women believe discussed in chapter two. Sometimes women assume that because they have not found a good man in the past and can't seem to find one now he must not exist. This position is based on limited knowledge. The fact is there are fifty-six million more men on this earth than women. Looking at those numbers a man could argue the difficulty in finding a virtuous woman, since there are fifty-six million fewer women.

It is true that good men are rare and uncommon, but so are virtuous women. Anything too common loses value. The unfortunate reality is women often look at men through the lens of past hurt. Without realizing it they punish a good man for what another man did to them. Punishing a man for another man's faults is a great disrespect to him. Respect is what every man wants. Just like women want security, men want respect. If a man is in your life in any capacity, you should respect him whether you think he deserves it or not. Always remember ladies, you cannot please a man without respecting him. If a good man is considering which of two women to date, when both are attractive to him, the level of genuine respect and honor a woman displays normally becomes the distinguishing factor.

Esther is the second woman in the Bible with a book named after her. She is an excellent example of showing respect and honor to the men in her life, therefore setting herself apart from other women. She was an orphan and adopted by her cousin Mordecai. Mordecai was a man of God and taught Esther the ways of the Lord. She was entered into a beauty contest that covered the whole empire because the king was looking for his queen. Hundreds of the most beautiful women in the world were competing for the affection of one man. This sounds like a great reality show! The women who were selected had to prepare for one year before they even had the opportunity to meet the king. Once they met him, they each had one night with him. They had one shot, one night with the king to prove themselves worthy of being his queen.

It was going to take more than just a beautiful face and great body to be named queen. All the women selected had world class beauty, so it could not just be looks. It also had to be more than their skills in the bedroom because they were all trained and prepared for a year before their one night. Just giving the king an orgasm was not enough to earn the honor of being queen.

The man in charge of keeping the women was a high ranking official called a eunuch. This means that he was castrated so he could not have sexual relations with the women in his care. Of all the women competing, Esther found favor with this eunuch. It was not her beauty that earned her favor because there were hundreds of beautiful women. It was not her sensuality that earned her favor because this man was a eunuch. Her wise words, good behavior, godly conduct, and the respect and honor she showed him earned her favor. As a result, she received privileges the other women did not. She was given a greater portion of beauty allowances than the other women and seven maidservants to assist her. The eunuch also moved her to the best place in the house. He no doubt told her some things the king liked and did not like to help her when she got her chance. When it was Esther's time to be with the king, he chose her as his queen.

Just like Esther, a woman today must be virtuous. She must learn how to distinguish herself from other women. A woman's body can please a man for the moment, but the respect she shows him will please him at all times. Good men are rare, but there are many good men. No man is born a good man; he must become a good man. Just like a woman must become virtuous. She is not born that way. That is why we must train our sons and daughters to be good men and virtuous women. The world needs them both desperately.

When women are discouraged, there is this evil little voice that continuously tells them they'll never have anyone. Then they see friends get married and rub it in their faces. Intentionally or unintentionally, their married friends seem to flaunt their husbands, rings, and marital success. Therefore, they often complain that all the good men are taken. No they are not! God is producing good men all the time! Never just settle for any man, even a "nice guy," when God is preparing a good man just for you.

Many men reading this book may have once been a rotten grape, but are now transformed into a plump juicy grape ready to be harvested! God is the transformer of bad men. He is taking scabs and making kings. He is taking the trash of the earth and making them treasures! The good man factory is producing them all the time. If you are a man reading this, allow the master to transform you into a good man, regardless of what you were before. We were all jacked up at one point, but don't stay there. Allow the work of God to continue until you are a good man. Stay connected to the vine and you will be ripe and fit to be used. This world desperately needs you!

Ladies please, don't ever pluck a man until he is juicy and ripe. If you pluck him while he is rotten on the vine, he will do nothing but get more rotten. Leave him on the vine and let God deal with him; you can't. As a matter of fact, many of a single woman's friends who got married, plucked a rotten grape from the vine, hoping it would ripen once she got it. A look at divorce court reveals that sometimes one or both of them were rotten or weren't ripe enough. Single women look at it this way; the married women who were not patient took all the rotten grapes off the vine for you so those who are left are the ones being ripened for harvest!

Every single woman reading this book must be patient. Impatience breeds desperation and desperation leads to bad decisions. Don't make the mistake of believing that patience is a passive word. Patience is very active.

While a single woman or man is being patient they are being ripened. The same good man factory that is putting out good men is churning out virtuous women. Patience gives the factory time to ripen them into a plump juicy grape. And every plump juicy grape wants one that is also juicy and ripe as well.

There was a woman in our church some years ago who directed our youth department. She did a great job for years. During that time I never saw her get fretful over not being married. She waited patiently for the Lord. As her pastor and spiritual father, I gave her some tough counsel regarding her preparation for getting a good man. This counsel was not because of any sinful areas in her life or because she had any major issues. The counsel I gave her was strictly about her physical appearance. I instructed her to be more conscious about how she looked when she went out of the house. Her hair, make-up, and clothing needed to be nice and vibrant all the time. It was tough for her because she had the habit of presenting herself a certain way. While the way she was presenting herself was not awful, it was not conducive to getting the attention of a good man. She was very plain, wore very little make-up, and wore very bland colors.

Remember ladies, no matter how spiritual a man is, every man walks by sight! We are visual beings. God made us that way and there is nothing you can do to change that. Looks are most important to a man. Whether you believe that to be shallow or not, it is a fact that has not changed since the first man walked on earth. Your inner beauty will never be seen if it is hidden behind the mask of plain and simple. The first way into a man's heart is through his eyes. If you can't get his attention, you cannot get his heart. Needless to say, I would never encourage a woman to dress sleazy or seductive. This attracts a certain type of man and repels the right type of man. All men may look at a provocatively dressed woman, but the good men will keep on walking.

I told my spiritual daughter to be made up and beautiful at all times. I told her firmly and very straightly to never leave the house without looking her best. This was not to be mean or hurt her feelings, but I loved her as my daughter and wanted her to be blessed. Just like the burning bush was used to get Moses attention so God could speak to him, being beautiful will get a good man's attention and give God a chance to speak to him. Even if his manhood speaks to him before God does, at least there is a chance. It was tough for her because it required much of her time and effort before she saw any results. It was also against her personality to make herself up and dress vibrantly. She struggled at first being consistent in making herself look beautiful every time. But after I spoke to her again she became ridiculously consistent. She would not even make a quick run to the store without fixing herself up. Once she followed my instructions completely, within a few months she caught the eye of a good man. They met, dated, and were married a short time later. By her obedience to counsel and following instructions, God gave her a good man.

Impatience produces the mind set a single woman told me many years ago, "A piece of man is better than no man at all." That philosophy brings disaster every time. If you get a piece of man that's all you'll ever get - a piece of his time, a piece of his money, and a piece of his heart.

Patience gives a good man time to ripen. It also gives a woman a chance to develop into the virtuous woman fit for a good man. The good men have not vanished; they are just being prepared and repaired for the virtuous women on the other side of the factory.

Chapter 10

"A good man out of the good treasure of his heart brings forth good; and an evil man out of the evil treasure of his heart brings forth evil. For out of the abundance of the heart his mouth speaks."

Luke 6:45

There is a little rhyme kids sometimes say that goes like this, "Sticks and stones may break my bones but words will never hurt me." It rhymes and it's sweet but few things are further from the truth. There is another saying that is used by many adults. The saying, "Talk is cheap" is heard all the time. While the reason behind this statement is understandable, it is also untrue. The world we live in is shaped by words. God created the universe by the words from his mouth. Words are the expression of thoughts and feelings. Words have started wars and ended them. Every relationship begins or ends with words. There is no marriage proposal without words. There are no vows without words. Salvation in Christ requires words. Words are the window into the heart of every person.

When someone is arrested, by law they are read their rights. The first two rights read to them are as follows, "You have the right to remain silent. Anything you say can and will be used against you in a court of law." There are large numbers of people in prison today because they opened their mouths and said the wrong thing. During political campaigns there is a term called "message discipline." This simply means that no matter what a politician is asked they will always stay on message, regardless of what they really feel or really want to say. Many politicians have lost elections because they did not maintain message discipline and said something they should not have.

There is a term I have coined called "mouth discipline." This means that no matter how emotional the situation may be, the person never speaks out of place or out of order. Sometimes the only way to achieve this is with silence. I told our church some time ago I'm going to develop a Water of Life Muzzle. This muzzle is to be placed gently over the mouth as a reminder of mouth discipline. Mouth discipline is critical because wrong words can be apologized for but cannot be retracted. Even a good man and virtuous woman must exercise mouth discipline in emotional situations. The Bible says, "There is a time to keep silence and a time to speak." A wise person knows the difference. Mouth discipline must be used when emotions want to speak but wisdom says be silent. Remember, silence may be misunderstood, but can never be misquoted.

The occasion of this verse is also recorded in Matthew's version and is the only time Jesus uses the phrase "good man." It's worth noting that His only use of this phrase concerns the words that a person speaks. He goes on to say, "Out of the abundance of the heart the mouth speaks." This reveals that at some point whatever is in a person's heart in abundance will eventually come out. The key word here is abundance. Many things compete for the attention of our heart. We have the responsibility of putting the right things in it. By listening to a person long enough, the content of their heart is revealed. Sometimes in the midst of intense dialogue someone might utter, "You have to know my heart." The truth is, however, the heart is always known by the words that come out of a person's mouth.

Sometimes in anger, frustration, or pressure we say things that may not actually be what our heart is full of. (This is why I'm developing the Water of Life Muzzle.) Over time, however, the real heart will speak and be known. It's like tap water. If we turn on the hot water, whatever is in the hot water heater will come out. The supply pipe is connected to it. Sometimes it takes a while for the hot water to arrive but eventually it does. The words we speak are the same way. Our mouths are permanently piped directly to our heart. This is why there is really no way to separate the message from the messenger. People can hide it for a while or cover it up temporarily. But, sooner or later what's in a person's heart will come out.

Jesus' statement is one of the most obvious ways to recognize a good man. The words that come from a good man are noticeably different from the words that come from a man who is not a good man. The first major distinction that the mouth reveals is lying versus telling the truth. There is no trait that more closely resembles the devil than lying. He is called the father of lies. The entirety of the ills of humanity is rooted in lies. The word "devil" itself means "accuser." He accuses God and he accuses people, all of them lies. Lying is not an accident; it is a deliberate attempt at deception. There are no white lies, black lies, green, red, or polka dotted lies. A lie is just a lie.

The sin nature of a man produces a tendency to lie. Even a young child will lie when he thinks he is in trouble. Ask him if he got a cookie when he was not supposed to. He will lie and say no, yet, cookie crumbs are all over his mouth. We have to be taught to tell the truth. A liar can never be a good man or a virtuous woman until he or she allows God to change his or her heart. A liar is one who lies. There is no set number of lies a person must tell before they become a liar. Lying destroys trust and relationships. A person who lies is one who cannot be trusted in any way. If someone lies to their boss, their friend, or their parents, it is proof of a corrupt heart and they will lie to anyone.

I had a girlfriend one time who was a big time liar. She would lie without even thinking. She would tell obvious lies and contradict herself several times in the same conversation. Even when she was with my parents, she would lie regularly. Despite her lying, I continued to date her somehow believing that she would eventually do better. Sometimes, I heard what I wanted to hear, not what she actually said. Strong emotional connections make that easy to do.

Lying is not just a personality defect; it's a major character flaw. I looked over my girlfriend's lies because she was fine and I wanted to be with her. This often happens when someone wants to be with a person so much that they ignore things they should not. My girlfriend's lying was not just red flags, but bombs going off and I still ignored it. I wanted her to be the right person so badly that I was oblivious to the person she really was. However, my desire for her to change could not make her change.

Some things should be non-negotiable for any relationship to continue. Telling the truth should be a non-negotiable and should never be compromised. Truth is the foundation for trust and a violation of trust corrupts the root of any relationship. Continuing in a relationship while tolerating lying is a recipe for disaster every time. The Lord bailed me out of that relationship. He pushed me out of the plane as it was going down and pulled my chute for me.

A good man has a good heart and it is revealed by his words. Someone who is not a good man will also reveal this by words. The Bible often uses the word "fruit" to describe someone's character. The primary way a tree is known is by its fruit. The only thing an apple tree can produce is apples because that's what it is. The only thing an orange tree can produce is oranges because that's what it is. No one can be fooled by any tree if they just look at its fruit. You can paint an apple orange and call it whatever you want in hopes of passing it off as an orange, but it is still an apple. The test for a good man or virtuous woman is no different; just like orange paint can only hide an apple for a moment, but the real fruit will soon be known. Patience is the key. Wrong people can say sweet things for a while, but patience will ultimately expose them.

The use of profanity is another very obvious character problem the mouth reveals; it exposes a heart that has profane things in it. I have an Xbox 360 and play video games online. The level of filth and profanity online is indescribable. Even children who play games online use the foulest language imaginable. While playing I have heard fathers curse their young children out using the most vile words. It really goes beyond just cursing, it's straight up cussin'! Nearly every time I play I have to turn down the earpiece volume so I can't hear it.

There are some who claim they only curse when they are angry or upset. They routinely play the "imperfection card" we discussed earlier. The real issue is not imperfection or simple mistakes, but a mouth that needs discipline and a heart that needs to change. Apologies are nice, but only genuine repentance brings a heart change. A changed heart is the only thing that can correct a foul mouth or lying lips. Words are released from the content of the heart; so, in order for words to change the heart must change. If the heart does not change, neither will the words.

There was a pastor many years ago that God allowed to have an experience with hell. God allowed him to be taken there one night and he described the experience. He said he was in a dark cell with demons taunting him and cursing him. He said even though he knew he was saved he started to panic. He ran to the wall and tried to climb out but it was slimy and his hands kept sliding off. He recalled the hideous red eyes of the demons in the cell with him. They said to him, "Didn't you hear about the Messiah? You are a fool for coming down here. We are going to torment you for all eternity." He then described how they cursed him using the vilest language.

Some words the demons cursed with he knew, some he didn't. As he recounted the experience, he noted the extreme profanity used by the demons and made it very clear all foul language comes from hell.

Experienced men know women respond to words. Because of this, flattery is the order of the day for a man trying to get into a woman's panties. A man of the world will say anything that will work. Just as men respond to sight, women respond to words. When I was in college I saw the men who were juniors and seniors look at the freshman women like steak. They marinated that steak with flattery and kind words and then smoked it. The freshman women were just excited that upperclassmen paid attention to them. They basked in the multitude of compliments without even noticing that their clothes were coming off. Adding alcohol to this equation made it work for those men just about every time. The naiveté of those freshman women, however, did not allow them to see that flattery as nothing more than lies wrapped in candy and a tool of deceit. Genuine compliments should be used generously, but flattery is a cloak of wrong motives.

Even without the use of profanity, words can still be most destructive. Many people have been told by mothers, fathers, relatives, friends, spouses, or others that they are worthless and will never amount to anything. Some were told this as children in the most harsh and abusive way. Many of you reading this book have experienced this. This type of abuse is diabolical and evil. It's important for you to know that those tirades directed toward you were nothing more than lies. Jesus is the healer and transformer of hearts. His word about you is what's true and His alone. Your greatness has been determined by your Creator, not by the ignorance of those who cannot recognize it. If this is you, surround yourself with people who encourage you. Learn what God says about you and pursue that reality. Your future is too bright to waste it with people who cannot discern your worth.

The heart of a person is known by their words. This is one of the easiest ways to distinguish a good man versus one who is not. Lying, profanity, and verbal abuse are not part of the character of a good man. A good man is full of good words because his heart is full of good things.

Chapter 11

"And, behold, there was a man named Joseph, a counsellor; and he was a good man, and a just."

Luke 23:50 KJV

Many years ago my pastor at the time ministered an awesome message called, "The Test That Most Christians Fail." I remember waiting to find out what this test was. Not only did I want to know what this test was, but I wanted to know why most Christians were failing it. If only a few people failed the test, you could say they were not prepared or there was a situation unique to them. But, when most people fail the same test, it is an indicator of a larger problem, not limited to an isolated case. I also wanted to know how the few who passed the test did it. If only a few pass this test, it was no accident and no fluke. They did what the others didn't and that's why they passed.

The test that most Christians fail is the fear of man and the fear of being talked about. Very few people will admit to being afraid of what people think or what people say about them; so the only way to really know is to observe their behavior. The evidence of the fear of man is not verbal admission but proven action.

We live in a culture that is obsessed with being politically correct. Nobody, especially the media, will call anything wrong for fear of offending someone. The philosophy of neutrality is evident everywhere. The notion of there being an absolute wrong and absolute right is shunned and avoided in our time. Those who do take a stand, especially on godly or moral issues, set themselves up to be a target. This is one of the reasons why many Christians during our time are afraid. It's tough being attacked with words and it's tough to be talked about. It's not easy to stand for what is right when the majority disagrees. This is why only a few pass this test. The heat of scrutiny causes many people to cave in under the pressure and weight of the majority opinion.

The main issue with this philosophy of neutrality is not the valid recognition of two equal opinions but the refusal to stand for truth which surpasses opinion and has no equal. So when someone under the risk of personal reputation, extreme criticism, or bodily harm stands up for what is right, it is worthy of honor. Most Christians won't do that.

This is the second verse in the Bible where the phrase good man is attached to an individual person. The first one was Ahimaaz discussed in chapter three. Joseph of Arimathaea is the man in this verse and is the first man in the New Testament called a good man. Because people in Bible days did not have last names, their occupation or where they were from was attached to their name. Arimathaea was where Joseph was from, so he can be distinguished from all the other Josephs. The Bible says he was a good man and a just man. While the focus of this book is the phrase "good man," the fact the Bible also calls him "just" is worth noting. The word translated "just" here means observing divine laws, upright, keeping the commands of God. The Bible's descriptions of people are always uncensored and unbiased. So, when he is called "a good man and a just," make no mistake, that's what he was.

The time of this verse is right after the crucifixion of Jesus. Joseph of Arimathaea was a wealthy and influential man during the time of Christ. He served on the 70 member council of the Jews called the Sanhedrin. The Sanhedrin was very powerful even though the country was under Roman rule. It was this council that voted to crucify

Jesus. The Sanhedrin was made up of the priest, religious leaders, and wealthy, prominent members of the Jewish community. The majority of men on this council hated Jesus because he threatened the power and influence they held. Many of them were the worst religious hypocrites of all time. They will be forever remembered as the council that sentenced to death the only sinless man to ever walk the earth. They knew Jesus was the Savior of the world, yet they did everything they could to destroy Him. Even the powerful Romans conceded to their wishes in condemning Jesus to death.

Joseph, though a member of this council, was a disciple of Jesus. His following of Jesus would have been very unpopular with his fellow Jewish constituents on the council because they hated Him. Joseph did not waver in his love for Jesus and did not back down from serving Him, even though it was unpopular. The high Jewish council hated Jesus and the Romans were afraid of him. The gullible Jewish populace were tricked and cried out for His death. But, Joseph would not back down. The Bible says he did not consent to the council's ruling to crucify Jesus. One can only imagine the type of pressure Joseph was under. The council wanted Jesus dead, the Romans wanted Him gone, and the Jewish people were shouting, "Crucify Him." Yet, Joseph stands up and says no. This is why the Bible calls him "a good man and just."

Crucifixion was one of the cruelest ways for a person to die. It was designed to kill slowly with maximum pain. Our word "excruciating" literally means the pains of crucifixion. This type of death was reserved for only the worst criminals. A Roman citizen could not be crucified. Sometimes the victim's body would be allowed to rot on the cross in disgrace. When they were buried, it was a common criminal's burial. Joseph would not allow his Lord to be so dishonored. He went to the Romans and boldly asked for the body of Jesus. He put Jesus in a tomb that he had purchased for himself. This was not a cave, but a tomb that had been carved out of rock. He paid to have this done so that when he died he would be buried there.

Not only was Joseph a good man but he was a man of great faith. He put Jesus in the tomb he had dug for himself; yet, there is no record that he had any plans for digging another one. Jesus said many times He would rise from the dead. This is why the Romans set guards at His tomb and put the seal of Rome over it. Breaking that seal meant death. Joseph knew Jesus was going to rise from the dead and his greatest act of faith was to allow Jesus to borrow his tomb for three days, knowing that he would not need it long. He had no plans to dig another tomb because he knew that he did not need to.

Having the guts and boldness to stand up for what is right are traits that a good man will possess. A good man does not punk out just because the majority believes differently. He boldly stands for truth regardless of what other people think or think about him. This does not mean he is stubborn and unyielding; a good man knows no one opinion carries more weight than another. When it comes to truth, however, and his conviction of it, he won't bend. A good man knows truth is not relative and is not multiple choice. He only compromises on differences of opinion, not differences of truth. He does not fear man but fears God and will not betray the truth of that conviction. Just like Joseph of Arimathaea, he stands for what is right.

During my junior year in college, I took over a Christian fellowship on campus. The previous leader turned it over to me without a vote or discussion. He felt very strongly God wanted him to appoint me. When he turned it over to me I was not second in command. I was not even third. I wasn't even officially licensed for ministry at the time. Despite that, I was promoted to the top above the second and third leaders, as well as licensed ministers also in the fellowship. It was a great honor and I accepted the challenge.

Shortly after I was appointed, I was asked to bring back a guest speaker who had ministered the previous semester. Everyone wanted him back and was looking forward to it. However, I had major issues and disagreements with this minister. His teaching on Bible prophecy was inaccurate and erroneous. I knew this because I had studied Bible prophecy for some time and I knew he was wrong to call a current U.S. leader the antichrist. The previous two leaders of the fellowship, the licensed ministers, and the entire group wanted to hear him again. I could not in good conscience, however, bring him back.

I wanted to do a good job and did not want to start off my ministry by ruffling feathers, but I could not betray the truth or the convictions I held. If I did, where would that compromise lead to and where would it end? I was the leader and held responsible for what the people were taught. If I compromised and agreed to something I knew to be wrong just to make people happy, how could I be trusted as a strong leader? I went to the previous leaders and told them I could not have him back and why. To my surprise, they had even greater respect for me as a result of my standing for what was right. God taught me in the genesis of my ministry that good men never compromise truth, even in the face of consequences.

In chapter five I quoted Dr. Martin Luther King and it bears repeating. He said, "The ultimate measure of a man is not where he stands in times of comfort and convenience, but where he stands in times of challenge and controversy." A good man stands with truth and lets the chips fall where they may. The size and strength of a man's muscles do not make the man. The size of a man's bank account does not make the man. Charisma and sex appeal do not make the man. What makes a man is his conviction of truth and his ability to stand on it. Dr. Martin Luther King also said, "History will have to record that the greatest tragedy of this time of social transition is not the strident clamor of the bad people, but the appalling silence of the good people." It was that same test most Christians fail that caused men to be silent when the voice of truth needed to be heard during Dr. King's time. There is no difference today. The fear of man still causes the appalling silence of unspoken truth.

Joseph of Arimathaea did not allow fear to drown the voice of truth. He stood up for truth and stood by his Lord during difficult days. Joseph passed the test that most Christians fail and earned forever the title "good man."

Chapter 12

"And there was much murmuring among the people concerning him: for some said, He is a good man: others said, Nay; but he deceiveth the people."

John 7:12 KJV

One of the things I ask the single men and women of our church is, "How much would it have been worth to you for somebody to have told you ahead of time that your worst relationship would end the way it did?" I ask them how much they would have paid for someone to warn them ahead of time about the hurt and pain of a bad relationship before the first date. Most of them admitted they would have paid anything for that foreknowledge. (I don't ask married people because their current spouse might be the source of their pain and regret.) The wisdom in this book is that foreknowledge. It is the biblical measuring stick for a good man. The right man will always measure up and the wrong one never will.

This verse records the comments of the people in Jesus' day about who He really was. There was murmuring and complaining about Him, and sometimes, straight up anger about who they perceived Jesus to be.

Was He a prophet, God, or just a good man as some of them contended? That debate still rages in our time and culture. Using the name of God in virtually any setting doesn't cause much of a stir; but using the name **JESUS** offends many people. The truth is, however, there is salvation in no other name but Jesus. The Bible calls Him a "rock of offense." No other person in history has been a greater rock of offense than Jesus. The moral standard of His absolute truth is a stumbling block to many.

On one occasion, Jesus asked His own disciples "Who do you say that I am?" Peter boldly declared, "You are the Christ, the Son of the living God." The settlement of who Jesus is in a person's life makes all the difference. A good man has settled in his heart and, like Peter, has concluded that Jesus is the Christ. Further than that, he has decided to invite Jesus into his heart. That acceptance transforms him into a Christian; one who is like Christ. This is the first way to define the word "good" in good man.

The challenge that often faces single men and single women is making sure that any person entering their lives does not occupy the wrong place in their hearts. In the zeal and excitement about a new or growing relationship, it becomes easy to give that person the throne of their heart that only God should have. The Lord is the only one in our lives that should always be first. Even after marriage, a spouse is always second to God. While this truth is often acknowledged, remember the evidence that the truth is really believed is the behavior that follows. No one should ever compromise their relationship with God for the relationship with another.

One of the most ironic twists in relationships between men and women is the attraction many women have for "bad boys." This is the type of man mothers want their daughters to avoid and fathers want to protect them from. Everything about these "bad boys" says "beware" or "run," yet many women have a strong attraction to these men. The arrogance, cockiness, rebellion, and recklessness male machoism that characterizes "bad boy" types are nothing like what most women say they want in a man. Most women say they want a man who is attractive, trustworthy, confident, financially stable, and has a sense of humor. Yet, despite their stated desires, they somehow end up seeing a bad boy.

According to a study by Harlequin Publishers, of nearly 1000 US women, 21% of women 35 and older said they would rather take a chance on a "bad boy" than date someone slow and steady. Thirty-one percent of women with children under the age of 18 would take a chance with a "bad boy." It is a fact these are the types of men who lie to, cuss out, abuse, and cheat on nearly every woman they are with. Relationships with "bad boys" end badly almost 100% of the time. Why would any woman want a man associated with the two words that bring her the most pain and frustration, "bad" and "boy?" Both words have heartache and headache written all over them. The "bad" brings the heartache and the "boy" brings the headache. "Bad boy" is the polar opposite of "good man".

Many of the attractive traits in so called "bad boys" are found in good men as well. They are confident, strong, and adventurous. The unfortunate reality is women have been ruined trying to salvage a bad boy and missed out on a good man. Some women subscribe to the philosophy that "nice guys finish last." This statement is not true. Every "nice guy" is not a "good man," but every "good man" is a "nice guy." A good man is a real man, not a wimp or punk. Good men have confidence, just not arrogance; never confuse the two. Good men put their foot down when needed, but won't beat a woman's head in when angry.

Good men are adventurous but not reckless. They are powerful, just not profane. Good men are rugged but not rebellious.

If you are a man reading this book it is important to know why women seem to be turned off by "nice guys." Women want a man, not a puppy, wimp, jelly back, or passive excuse for a man. Learn how to be assertive, aggressive, and confident. Don't just go along with anything and everything just to keep peace when you disagree and know it's wrong. This does not mean be stubborn and hard to deal with, but it does mean be a man and be strong. Don't apologize for being manly. Strengthen that spine that God gave you. No woman wants a push over or puppy dog they have to drag along. In chapter five, we talked about the manhood of Jesus. It's not sinful or wrong to act like there is some testosterone running through your veins. God gave it to you; it's what makes you a man.

Many young and older women get sucked in by this bad boy persona. The disastrous attraction to the "thug" type of guy can cost a woman years of heartache and headache. There is nothing good about a "thug". The word "thug" means deceive, sly, fraudulent, dishonest, scoundrel, one who conceals. Thugs were a particular type of murderer in South Asia, mainly in India, hundreds of years ago. They would gain the trust of a caravan of travelers by joining them and pretending to be travelers themselves. Sometimes they would travel for days and hundreds of miles with the caravan. They often promised the travelers unity and protection. Once the thugs gained their trust and the travelers let their guard down, the thugs located a place suitable to prevent escape and away from local observers. The thugs then killed and robbed the travelers. Their preferred method of execution was strangulation. It was quick, quiet, and left no stains. When the British colonized India, they encountered these thugs and the term is still used today.

The only difference today with our modern understanding of the word "thug" is that not all thugs are mass murderers (though some still are). They are still deceptive, sly, dishonest scoundrels most of the time. They still lure people with kind words and promises of unity and protection while planning to do them harm when the time is right. They are liars, rebellious, profane, and only think of themselves. They are arrogant, stubborn, and often violent. They have the same spirit as the original thugs and can never be trusted. Nothing good comes from association with a thug.

For any woman reading this book that seems to be attracted to the bad boy, thug, gangsta, goon, or the like, this is the warning about the hurt and pain a relationship with them will cause you. Don't even get into the relationship. Run for your life! Use the standards in this book and allow God to give you a good man. The more time you waste messing with a bad boy or thug adds to the time it takes a good man to find you. Not only that, when your emotions are strong for this type of man, you convince yourself to stay with him, even though you know it will end badly. Your emotions will not allow you to let him go. This is why it is so critical for a woman not to even enter the wrong relationship in the first place. The identification team we will discuss later will save you if you listen to them. If you are unmarried but already in a bad relationship, it's not too late. You must decide, however, to get out now. The temporary pain is much better than the long term misery.

More often than not when a woman is caught up with a bad boy or thug, a good man is within sight. She either can't see him or ignores him in her pursuit of the wrong man. She often labels him as dull, boring, and unmanly and won't even give him a chance. Sometimes the man of her dreams is within arm's reach, but she literally cannot see the forest for the trees.

There was a woman I liked many years ago. We were in school together and had some classes together. She was beautiful and fun to be around. I had thoughts of taking our friendship further, but she was in a bad relationship. Her boyfriend was abusive and beat her behind, yet she would not leave him. I never really pressed the issue about us with her because I knew she had a boyfriend. I never met him, but I saw the evidence of his presence from her black eye and bruises on her face. She dismissed the quality of our friendship as just that, a friendship. I was a nice guy, but not the image of the proverbial "nice guy." I was and still am 100% man, not a punk, wimp, or sissy. I have never been feminine, soft, passive, fearful, or weak. I was athletic and competitive, bold and confrontational. I said what I meant, I meant what I said, and I kept my word. But, I was no thug or bad boy. She overlooked a man who cared for her and was always there to stay with a man who whipped her butt.

This is why God says that sexual intimacy is just for marriage. Sexual intimacy creates a greater appetite for it and an emotional bond in women that is difficult to break. I can always tell if people are sleeping together because of their inability to separate from a bad relationship. Keeping the relationship pure invites God in and keeps emotions in line with wisdom, reason, objectivity, and good sense. With unmarried couples, the inability to pull away is proof of an unholy, sexual bond.

A heart like Christ is the definer of the word "good" in good man. It is one of the distinguishing traits between a woman and a virtuous woman. Though the debate about who Jesus is rages on in our time, for good men and virtuous women, there is no debate. Jesus is God and He is the Savior. Jesus is more than "a good man;" He is the maker of good men.

Chapter 13

"For he was a good man, full of the Holy Spirit and of faith. And a great many people were added to the Lord."

Acts 11:24

This is the third and last time the Bible uses the phrase good man to describe an individual person. Ahimaaz and Joseph of Arimathaea were the first two. The man this verse is talking about is Barnabas. As I mentioned earlier, when the Bible discusses a person's life, everything is exposed. All of the good and the bad are known and secrets revealed. So any assessment of a person's life is uncut, uncensored, and unbiased because it is authored by the Spirit of God.

The name Barnabas means "son of encouragement." It is worth noting this was not his birth name. This was a name given to him, similar to a nickname. His birth name was Joses, but he is only called by his birth name once in the Bible. The apostles gave him the name Barnabas because of his character, faith, heart of reconciliation, and sacrificial giving. Barnabas was a wealthy man and a tremendous giver which is one of the reasons he is called the "son of encouragement." He was not stingy, nor did he hoard his wealth, but sold some of his property and gave the profit to support the work of the Lord. He was a good friend and traveling companion of the great apostle Paul, whom God used to write two-thirds of the New Testament.

The Apostle Paul had a disturbing past. He persecuted and imprisoned many of God's people before his conversion to Christ. As a matter of fact, the first Christian martyr was Stephen and his blood stained clothes were laid at Saul's feet (The Apostle Paul's name before his conversion.) Once he was converted, the church did not readily accept him because they did not trust that he was really a Christian. It was Barnabas who brought Paul to the apostles and confirmed that he was genuinely converted. Because they trusted Barnabas, they accepted Paul. Without Barnabas who knows if the Apostle Paul would ever have been accepted by the apostles.

Barnabas was used by God to reconcile, restore, and unify. He also restored a man named John-Mark back into the ministry. John-Mark made some major mistakes in ministry and abandoned the work of the Lord on very important missionary trips. Some men of God did not want to take John-Mark with them anymore after that. Once he repented, however, Barnabas gave him another chance and he did not let them down. John-Mark was the man who wrote the Gospel of Mark that we have in our Bible. It is believed that Mark's Gospel was the first one written about the life and ministry of Jesus.

Barnabas and Paul were the two lead apostles sent on missionary journeys to bring the gospel to much of the known world at the time. Barnabas was a trusted and powerful servant of the Lord. He was most critical in the advancement of God's word in the early days of the church. One could argue we might not have the entirety of the New Testament we have today if it were not for Barnabas because he connected Paul with the other apostles and restored John-Mark. It was the character of Barnabas and his service to God that caused him to stand out, not his wealth.

Most women would love to have a man like Barnabas. But, some would value him more for his wealth than for his character. It is this misplaced value that keeps some women from attracting a good man. Good men notice wrong motives eventually and want nothing to do with them. Attempting to manipulate a good man or lure him into a sexual trap by trying to booty whip him normally backfires. While it may entice a good man, it will seldom retain him.

Prostitution is called the world's oldest profession, and no doubt it is. The question that begs to be asked is why? Why would women who sell their body for money be considered the oldest professionals known to man? A follow up question then would be why do men pay large sums of money to sleep with them? This is no doubt the greatest perversion of the relationship between men and women. I believe the answer to those questions lies in understanding the way God made us.

We were created by God and it is no accident He made us the way He did. The very first command God gave mankind was to "be fruitful and multiply." God designed us physically and emotionally so that obeying this command would be desirable. One of the reasons homosexuality is condemned by God is because it violates the first commandment given to man. Two women cannot multiply and two men cannot multiply. Their parts do not fit!

Not only did God make us physically different, but we are emotionally different and we think differently as well. We are intellectually equal but have different needs and desires. We discussed earlier that men have a need for respect and women for security. This is why one of the worst things a woman can do to a man is to disrespect and to dishonor him. It strips him of his ego and his manhood. Nearly every man will gravitate to a woman who honors him and respects him. If she makes him feel like a man, he wants to be around her. If she makes him feel like less than a man he will avoid her.

This is how a man can genuinely love his wife but sleep with another woman. He loves his wife but loves how he feels about himself when he is with the other woman. When he is with her he feels like a man. Any man who does this is still very wrong, but married women must understand this dynamic in a man. It is critical that she makes him feel like a man when he's with her. Obviously this is not the reason for every affair men have. Sometimes he's just a knucklehead and will not be faithful to his wife. However, a wife who strips her husband's manhood does reveal a contributing factor to how the "other woman" often slithers in.

Conversely, the worst thing a man can do to a woman is take away her security. She needs emotional and financial security. Stripping those things away from a woman strips the very core of her being. If a man provides a woman security, reassures her emotionally, and secures her financially, she will want to be with him because he is meeting her most important needs. This is why a lazy, non-working man is intolerable to many women. Not only does he not provide security but seems to have no ambition, to ever provide it. If he has drive and ambition there is at least the hope of future financial security and a woman sees that as attractive. Even though men have a natural instinct to protect and provide for the woman he loves, the emotional security she needs is something that most of us men have to learn to give. Be patient with us ladies, this does not always come naturally to us.

One thing that can cause a woman to settle for just any man is desperation. In some cases, the man has no money or job, has no drive or ambition, is ungodly and unrighteous, rejects God and won't listen to anyone. He has the ability to work but won't. Yet, a desperate woman will allow him to sit on her couch, lie in her bed, and play video games while she pays his bills. Ladies, please never allow that to happen! The fact you are reading this book indicates you want to know how to identify a good man.

It's also just as important to be able to recognize one who is not.

Those critical needs men and women have can also be counterfeited. A man may know a woman is only respecting him because of his money, but as long as he still feels respected and powerful he tolerates it. Even if a woman knows the only reason she is provided for is because she gives sexual favors, she may tolerate it because she still has financial security. This is how the pimp and prostitute have survived for thousands of years. One provides false respect, the other provides false security.

The reality is men want sex and women want love and affection. A man will give love and affection to get sex, and a woman will give sex to get love and affection. Testosterone makes a man sexually aggressive, so there is no doubt God intended the man to pursue. Not only that, but there is a physical build up of semen in men that occurs every three days. With that build up comes great pressure. If that semen is not released in 72 hours, a man is desperate to relieve the pressure. When you add the element of achievement to a man's sexual release, that makes for a very strong driving force. So married women, there is a hormonal, physical, and emotional reason your husband wants sex all the time. He's not crazy, he's just normal. That's why if you give a man of the world sex and money he is basically happy. I know it sounds shallow to women, but it is the truth. It takes more than that for true fulfillment in a man's life, but for simple happiness that's about it. Needless to say every man is different, but I believe this includes a large number of men.

Please notice in the last paragraph I addressed married women, husband and wife, not boyfriend and girlfriend, and not even fiancé. God commanded sexual needs to be met inside of marriage and no other place. Just because our society says it's alright for unmarried couples to sleep together or even live together does not change God's standard. God's blessing follows His standard, not the standard of society's opinion.

Emotion is the engine that drives women. If a woman is emotionally and financially secure she is basically happy. If a man provides both of them she feels free to give herself to him. If any one of those goes lacking, it throws her off. This is why the most beautiful women sometimes hook up with the most hideous men. If a man is ugly and wealthy, he's got a chance. If he's ugly and broke, forget it! (Unless, of course, she is desperate to be with someone as we just discussed.) He may be ugly, but if he provides emotional and financial security that's two out of three and she will give him a second look. If a man meets those two needs for a woman, she can learn to love him.

Over time, this meeting of needs between men and women has taken on many different perversions. The reason some women tend to run after professional athletes is primarily because of the financial provision they can provide. Tons of women, often called "groupies," find out where the athletes stay when they travel, go to clubs they frequent, dress themselves provocatively, and try to lure them in. The muscular stature of an athlete's physique is an added bonus. The same holds true for actors, singers, musicians, and other celebrities. The wealth of these men does not make them good just like it was not the wealth of Barnabas that made him good. It was his faith, character, and service to the God that made him good.

These wealthy male celebrities often sleep with as many of those "groupies" as they can. You never hear about, however, celebrity women sleeping with male groupies. Men who follow celebrity women are not called groupies but stalkers. They follow beautiful celebrity women and often film them or take pictures of them. "Groupies" seldom go to jail, but stalking is a crime and stalkers go to jail. Stalkers are considered crazy and dangerous, and they are. But, in reality, some of those groupies are just as crazy and just as dangerous.

An exception to this is the success of the gigolo. Wealthy women will often pay for the romance, sexual services, and companionship of a man. Simply put, a gigolo is a male prostitute sometimes called a male escort. The gigolo is not a stalker but a professional stud who positions himself as the object of a woman's desire. With sex as the basis for this relationship and money being the medium of exchange, it is another perverse way of meeting needs.

The "sugar daddy" is another perversion of meeting needs. A "sugar daddy" is a man who has one or more women he financially cares for. In exchange for his provision, she gives him sex as frequently as he wants. He is not a good man and the epitome of one to avoid. However, there are times, if the woman has children and a low income, the only way she sees her needs can be met is by this man. So, she tolerates his foolish behavior and sometimes abuse because she knows he pays her bills. She compromises every ounce of her morals and integrity to meet a few needs and have a little money. If he pretends to be "daddy," she'll provide him the "sugar." If you are a woman reading this and this scenario describes you, there is hope. Get rid of the "sugar daddy" and seek your Heavenly Father and trust Him to provide for you. Not only will He provide for you, but he will affirm your greatness and give you a good man at the right time because He really loves you!

There is a phrase that describes another one of these perversions called "gold diggers." While both men and women can "gold dig," a man who does cannot be described in two words. He is basically a lazy, worthless, good for nothing, pathetic excuse for a man. While that sounds harsh, it's true. A man who does this has rejected the dignity of manhood. The difference between a woman gold digger and one with a sugar daddy is a gold digger can normally support herself; she just has a craving for more. Her materialism causes her to sell her soul, body, or anything else she has to get the stuff she wants. She cares nothing about the man being good, bad, ugly, or a thug, as long as he has money and is willing to spend it on her.

During some foolish days of my life I used this perversion of needs to my advantage. I knew many women who had children and no employment. As a result, they lived in certain neighborhoods where poverty was the norm. I was not wealthy, but because of where I lived and what I drove, it gave the illusion that I had more than what I had. I didn't intentionally perpetrate, but I did not say otherwise either. I would sleep with those women as much as possible but never took them anywhere. There were several women with whom I had that "arrangement." As I said earlier, I didn't try to hurt them, nor was I mean or abusive. But, I was selfish and I wanted what I wanted. Some of these women were Christian women who went to church, but I knew what they did after church and what they did the Saturday night before. Their needs and desires surpassed their commitment to God. Quite frankly, I was worse.

Whether you are a man or woman reading this book, it is proof you treasure wisdom and would not be like any of the men and women just described. Equally important again is the ability to recognize those who are and avoid them. If you are like the people just described, or like I used to be, Jesus is the transformer of hearts, and if you give Him yours He will transform it.

It takes strength, character, and the help of God for a man not to look at a woman's body and a woman not to look at a man's money as the basis of any relationship. Good men and virtuous women meet those needs in the confines of a holy marriage, not the multiple perversions outside of it.

Barnabas was a wealthy man, but his wealth and social status had nothing to do with his title "good man." His giving did not define his character, it reflected it. In other words, he was a giver because he was a good man, not a good man because he was a giver. He wasn't a humanitarian; he was a servant of the Lord. Good deeds do not make a man a good man. It is the character of his being that makes him one. The faith of Barnabas, his heart of reconciliation and restoration, his ability to unify, and the fullness of God's Spirit in him, earned him the title good man. When those traits are valued by a man, it drives him to become a good man. When they are valued by a woman, she becomes irresistible to a good man.

Chapter 14

"For scarcely for a righteous man will one die; yet perhaps for a good man someone would even dare to die."

Romans 5:7

I think it is fitting that the last place in the Bible that records the phrase "good man" describes the depth of mercy and grace that God has shown us. We have covered nearly a dozen verses that describe in detail the character of a good man. Now, at the end, the Bible lets us know that perhaps someone might consider dying for a good man. However, Jesus died for us while we were still in our mess.

As I said earlier, no man was born a good man; he must become a good man. No woman was born a virtuous woman; she must become a virtuous woman. Even when we were no good, Jesus died for us so we could become good. The will to make the necessary changes to become what we need to be is critical. The word "will" is key. So often a man or woman may know what he or she needs to do to improve but won't do it. They may know what is right but refuse to live it. God is sovereign and has all power to do anything He wants. However, He has given man sovereignty over his own will.

Contrary to popular opinion, when something good or bad happens it was not necessarily God's will. We often hear people say, "Well, if it's God's will it's going to happen," or "It must be God's will or it would not have happened." Those statements sound good, but they are not true. Many times we make or cause things to happen that were never in God's will. Because God has given us sovereignty over our own will, many things that happen in our lives are the result of what we wanted to happen.

God never has and never will make us serve or obey Him. If we choose to walk in His will, then our will is lined with God's will. A perfect harmony of wills brings in our lives the greatest fruit of significance and joy. On the other hand, if we decide to do what we want, God will let us. If we rebel and choose a contrary path, He will not stop us. Though we have the sovereignty over our will, we do not have control over the consequences of our decisions. God has promised blessings for obedience and consequences for disobedience; we must decide.

This applies to relationships as well. Sometimes we want a relationship to be God's will so badly we force it and then erroneously conclude that if it is not God's will it will never work. During some past years of my life, I was an expert in making something work that was not God's will. I hoped, prayed, and tried to make it be God's will or at least change His mind about it. I allowed the strong emotions I had for the woman, to override the will of God, wisdom, and sometimes even common sense.

The word emotion means to move. Emotions can move us to make bad decisions. That's why the Bible never tells us to follow them. As a matter of fact, the Bible says, "a fool trusts in his own heart." The popular phrase "do what feels right" has gotten a lot of people in trouble. While having a gut feeling about something has merit at times, God tells us to be led by the Spirit. This is why patience and counsel are always wise before entering relationships because they can give us the opportunity for discernment before emotions come into play.

There is a verse I always use when my wife and I perform wedding ceremonies and it says, "Unless the Lord builds the house they labor in vain who build it." This verse is often used during building projects for churches. While it is alright to use it for that, it really refers to the building of an individual household. It doesn't refer to the brick and mortar dwelling place, rather the family who lives in it.

In this nation, there are many people building families the Lord is not building. The Bible did not say it could not or would not be built. It just says unless the Lord does it, the house will be built in vain. For God to build a house He must not only be the builder, but the architect and engineer as well. God will only build a house according to His design. But, His building the house is based on the cooperation of those who want it built.

The reason many of my relationships in the past were not God's will was, first of all, the woman I wanted was not the one God destined for me. Secondly, there was a conflict of wills. Neither of us was willing to cooperate with God's plan for our lives at the time. My desperation to make it God's will did not change God's mind, nor did it change the heart and will of either of us. Our unwillingness to cooperate with the will of God was the principal reason God's blessing was not on the relationship. The conflict of wills we both had with God's will would have ultimately landed us both in a place in life we did not want to be.

God is so merciful and He has had as much mercy on me as anyone. His mercy and grace are everlasting and the proof was His willingness to sacrifice Himself for us when no one was good. Now, because of His sacrifice, any man can become a good man and any woman can become a virtuous woman. Not only that, His word has given us the ability to identify those who are.

Chapter 15

We have covered every verse in the Bible that uses the phrase "good man." From those verses we have constructed God's standard for what a good man is. Even though we have covered these verses in detail, every virtuous single woman still should have an identification team. In other words, there ought to be some people around her who can help her identify when she has been found by a good man. When the standard for a good man is unknown it is almost impossible to identify him. If someone says, "Go outside and when you see it let me know," the first question then becomes, "See what?" Even though we now know the standards for a good man, the identification team helps to make a positive I.D. In our justice system, a positive identification must be made of a person on trial in a court of law. There are fingerprints and DNA testing which prove a person's identification. Only by the help of God and a woman's identification team can a positive I.D. be made of a good man.

A single woman should never get advice (as we discussed earlier); she needs counsel. If a good man has found a virtuous woman, he will pass the test of validation by her team.

One of the biggest mistakes many women make is listening to the wrong people or no one at all. So often worldly, ungodly advice is given on how to win and keep a man. In most instances, this advice attracts the wrong attention and the wrong man. This always brings grief. You'll find in these situations the relationship is hidden because she knows her identification team will not approve. A woman never has to hide someone God has given her. Proceeding without authentication by her team will result in relationship mistakes. Impatience, desperation, or outright rebellion are the reasons a woman will pursue a relationship without authentication by her team. This can lead to irrational and reckless decisions. Severe consequences and emotional ruin are sure to follow.

In this case, a man could be an axe murderer wanted in all fifty states. But, if a woman's emotions are out of control, she will lay aside all reason, defend him, and fool herself into thinking there is nothing wrong with him. Even if she is saved and filled with the Spirit of God, she needs a team to help her identify a good man.

Who should be on a woman's identification team:

1.   Her father if he is living and a godly man.

The reason a woman's father is so important is because a father is the first male authority in a woman's life. In Bible days, the groom would negotiate a dowry, or a form of payment, for the opportunity to marry a man's daughter. The father had the choice whether or not to accept the dowry. It was also his choice whether to give his blessing or not. The dowry was proof to the father the groom could provide for his daughter and compensated him for the loss of her labor.

In our time and culture, that seems crude and demeaning, but it assured her financial support. A woman's financial support in Bible days was critical because they could not work like women in our culture today. This also protected her against marrying the wrong man. It is important to note that in Bible days a woman would not marry someone her father did not approve. The father's blessing was most important when it came to a person's inheritance, as well as their marriage. The father's blessing was a must. God honored the father's blessing as though He himself had given it.

Though we live in modern times, God has not changed His standard of the father's blessing. He still honors the father's blessing as though He gave it Himself. The difficulty with our time and culture is there are many fathers who have not lived up to their mandate from God for their children. They have not served Him and many have abused, abandoned, or neglected their children and their wives. In these cases, it is extremely difficult for a daughter to respect, much less ask for, her father's blessing.

I believe in such a situation God uses a woman's spiritual father, which could be her pastor, to provide the needed blessing. (We'll cover that when we discuss the next member of the team.) If the father has passed away, a stepfather, spiritual father, or other godly, male authority figure in her life could fill that role. The blessing makes all the difference. The blessing is that divine energy and empowerment which causes what we do to prosper. Without the blessing, the grief and pain of failure are sure. It is a statistical fact that 80% of marriages that begin at the courthouse end at the courthouse in divorce. There are a number of reasons for this. I believe the main reason is most of those marriages start in rebellion without the father's blessing. It is clear the blessing comes through the father; never violate that.

2.   Her pastor, if she does not have a pastor she should get into a good church and get to know the pastor and he get to know her.

In our culture and time, men of God do not get the respect God commanded is due to them. Servants of God are ridiculed, made fun of, and are never shown in a good light in movies or television. While it is true that many servants of God have fallen, failed, or not lived up to their calling, the vast majority of God's servants, while imperfect, walk upright and with integrity. The sacrifices these servants of God make to do his will may never be known fully by anyone but God. The fact is, however, even with their imperfection, God still requires us to honor His servants. God honors those who honor His servants. Every virtuous woman should have a pastor, not just someone who preaches at the church she attends.

A pastor has the mandate to watch out for souls of the people God has placed under him. God never violates our will, so submission to pastoral authority is voluntary. Quite frankly, submission to God is voluntary as well. We decide to follow or not. But, we do not decide the consequences of our decisions. Just like a human shepherd, a pastor knows the personality, strengths, and weaknesses of his sheep. A real shepherd loves and cares for the sheep. A human shepherd has the same love and responsibility towards human sheep. This is why a virtuous woman should be in a good church and have a pastor who knows and cares for her. One of the characteristics of shepherds is they can see much better and much further than the sheep. This is true of a human shepherd or pastor as well. Human sheep must trust the wisdom and foresight of their shepherds. This is the biblical principle called a covering. A covering shields and protects from anything that would do harm. A covering is also a shade of comfort from the heat and rain. God knew all of us needed that protection and that is why He commanded all of His people to have human shepherds.

Some make the mistake of assuming this type of covering is a form of control. There is no control in real submission. Real submission to authority is an act of our will, not an act of obligation. God commands all of us to submit to higher authority whether natural or spiritual; it is a canopy of protection.

The reward of submission is protection. Even in our country, we must submit to the authorities over us. We don't always agree with them, but the reward of submission is the protection our government, police, and military provide. The only real evidence of submission is obedience beyond the point of agreement. If we only obey what we agree with then there is really no submission. In that case we become our own authority. One great man of God put it this way, "Submission only begins when agreement ends." A virtuous woman should never connect emotionally to a man without validation from her covering. If she submits to this protection, it will save a woman many tears and bring a lot of smiles.

3.   *A godly, mature, stable, married woman in Christ with a happy godly man in Christ.*

The Bible tells the older women to teach the younger women good things. The older more mature women should be teaching the younger women how to be women of God, how to love their husbands if they are married, and how to be godly, virtuous, and upright. The mature women are to be an example in lifestyle to the younger women. The example of Naomi and Ruth in chapter two is a good illustration because Naomi gave Ruth wisdom and instruction which allowed her to win the heart of a good man. Unfortunately, in our country, wisdom does not always come with age; sometimes age comes all by itself. There are many older women who are just as foolish, silly, and naive as the younger women. The woman qualified to be on this team is a woman who has proven herself over time. This woman is virtuous herself and lives a godly lifestyle in and out of church. She is trusted by her pastor and under authority. She prays, does not gossip, is loving, is kind, and has a godly man herself if she is married. Not only that, but her husband is happy.

The Bible tells us to copy the behavior of those who through faith and patience inherit the promises. By copying a godly woman's behavior, a woman puts herself in position to get the same results. God has no respect of persons; He respects obedience and faithfulness. Far too often, women in our time listen to older women who are angry, bitter, or just unwise. Unfortunately, sometimes this is a woman's mother. While every mother deserves respect and honor just as any father, not every mother gives godly counsel. A virtuous woman must choose wisely the woman from whom she receives counsel. The value of this person on a woman's identification team is immense. This mature woman is not a friend but more of a mentor. One man of God put it this way, "A friend loves you the way you are. A mentor loves you too much to leave you the way you are."

It may be wise to ask your pastor for such a mentor in your life. Just like your pastor should know you, he should know this woman as well. Asking your pastor prevents you from choosing someone just because she is older, goes to church regularly, or has charisma. The pastor knows her character. Learning from the experiences of this woman of God will bring bountiful blessings to any young woman. Foolishness is having to make every mistake yourself. Wisdom is learning from the mistakes of others.

4. *Godly friends who love Jesus and live for Him.*

Choosing friends is critical to the future of anyone's life. Anytime someone fails, they do not fail alone. Someone influenced them in some way. Likewise, when someone succeeds, they don't do it alone. Some other person influenced them or helped them succeed. I heard someone put it like this, "There are four kinds of people in your life: those who add, those who subtract, those who multiply, and those who divide." Wrong people never exit your life voluntarily and the right people seldom enter your life accidentally. Wrong people must be put out and right people be brought in. People are catalysts; they are junction points moving you in a certain direction. There are no passive people in your life. They are either contributing to your success or aiding your failure. Time with people is either a good investment or a liability. Foolishness and drama always come along with the wrong people in your life.

The story of Jonah in the Bible is a classic case of this. Jonah refused to obey God's command to go to a certain city and minister to them. He did not like the people there because they were evil and brutal. So he decided to catch a boat in the opposite direction. While he was on the boat, a very strong storm came up. The experienced sailors did all they could to lighten the ship. They threw everything overboard but the storm still raged. Jonah knew he was the cause of the storm. It was not until they threw Jonah overboard that the storm ceased. He was then swallowed by a big fish and taken to where he should have gone anyway. The example here shows it is not what is on your ship but who is on your ship that makes the difference in your life. Throw Jonah overboard!

A virtuous woman must choose the right friends. These friends should be other women who are virtuous as well. They should serve the Lord fully and live an upright life in and out of church. The sitcom *Girlfriends* several years ago is not the standard for how virtuous women should be. Commitment to God and righteous living should be the minimum requirements for any women on this team. Furthermore, these women should display wisdom and discretion in the affairs of their own lives, have a pastor, and be under a covering themselves. If a woman does not meet these high standards, she should not be on a virtuous woman's identification team. If the wrong woman is on the team, she will be a negative influence when critical decisions must be made. The voice of ungodliness and worldly perspective should never be in the ears of a virtuous woman, no matter where it is coming from.

Every woman should have an identification team in place and not make any significant relationship decisions until the team validates the one in her life. A woman's father and pastor are the most important people on this team because they carry with them the God-honored blessing. She should never violate their counsel. Their wisdom, counsel, and protection are critical for her success. This team is not in a virtuous woman's life to invade her privacy or get in her business, but serves as an army of protection. Every virtuous woman is a treasure and only a good man is worthy to pass through this security to his treasure. A good man will understand and respect the protection this team provides.

The building is now complete and the question, "What is a good man?" has now been answered. The image of a good man is evident for everyone to see. Ideas, speculations, estimations, and opinions are no longer necessary. God has given us the standard by which men should measure themselves and the DNA criteria by which a woman can positively identify a good man. Any woman, who allows God to create grace and virtue within her, stands out as a gem among stones shining brightly for a good man to see.

The same God who created man perfect before his fall, through Christ, can recreate men who have fallen. This is why the Spirit of God is the irreplaceable ingredient of the word "good," in the phrase "good man." It distinguishes a "nice guy" from a "good man" and transcends noble, visible attributes and goes right to the heart of the matter. When a man allows God to recreate and develop him, he measures up to God's standard and earns the title "GOOD MAN."

CPSIA information can be obtained at www.ICGtesting.com
Printed in the USA
LVOW121655010312

271205LV00002B/4/P